SpringerBriefs in Law

For further volumes:
http://www.springer.com/series/10164

Olukunle Ola

Copyright Collective Administration in Nigeria

Lessons for Africa

Springer

Olukunle Ola
Faculty of Law
Australian Catholic University
Melbourne, VIC
Australia

ISSN 2192-855X ISSN 2192-8568 (electronic)
ISBN 978-3-642-35818-0 ISBN 978-3-642-35819-7 (eBook)
DOI 10.1007/978-3-642-35819-7
Springer Heidelberg New York Dordrecht London

Library of Congress Control Number: 2013930687

Printed on acid-free paper

Springer is part of Springer Science+Business Media (www.springer.com)

Preface

The introduction of a regulatory framework in the area of collective management of rights in Nigeria must have been intended to strengthen the creative industry. In some ways it may have done so but at the same time it has thrown the industry and in particular the music and film industries into a battle of *a regulated against a non-regulated* collective administration sector for upward of 20 years.

This book is a product of the interest I developed while administering the collective administration desk at the Nigerian Copyright Commission. Serving on that desk afforded the opportunity to delve into the realm of collective administration where I was able to observe the intrigues and the frustration of right owners who were being deprived the fruit of their labor, as the societies meant to collect and distribute royalties on their behalf were enmeshed in litigations and in the process, rarely paid any royalties to authors.

The question whether there is any merit in the continued existence of the current regulatory framework for collective management in Nigeria, and what the best operational framework for collective administration in Nigeria would be is considered in this work.

It is hoped that this research will spur a desire for the need for supervisory and regulatory agencies of government to seek the national interest above all others in taking and making decisions that affect the collective administration of copyright and related rights and indeed the general public.

Keywords Copyright and Related (Neighboring) Rights · Collective Administration · Collecting Society · Collective Management Organisations · Nigerian Copyright Commission · Musical Copyright Society Nigeria Limited by Guarantee · Owner, Assignee and Exclusive Licensee · Regulatory framework · Regulation · Musical works

Contents

Acronyms and Abbreviations

AMB PRO	Association of Music Business Professionals
ASCAP	The American Society of Composers Authors and Publishers
BMI	Broadcast Music Inc
CAMA	Companies and Allied Matters Act
CEO	Chief Executive Officer
CISAC	International Confederation of Societies of Authors and Composers
CMO	Collective Management Organisations
COLUM-VLA J.L. and ARTS	Columbia Journal of Law and the Arts
COSON	Copyright Society of Nigeria
GDP	Gross Domestic Product
GNI	Gross National Income
HDI	Human Development Index
IFPI	International Federation of Phonographic Industries
IFRRO	International Federation of Reproduction Rights Organisation
IP	Intellectual Property
MCPS	Mechanical Copyright Protection Society
MCSN	Musical Copyright Society Nigeria Ltd/Gte
MORAN	Music Label Owners & Recording Industries Association of Nigeria
NARI	Nigerian Association of Recording Industries
NCC	Nigerian Copyright Commission
NORM	National Organisation for Reproduction Rights in Music
N. Ky. L. Rev	The Northern Kentucky Law Review
PMAN	Performing Musicians Association of Nigeria
PMRS	Performing and Mechanical Rights Society of Nigeria Ltd/Gte
PRO's	Performing Rights Organisations
PRS	PRS for Music

PwC	PricewaterhouseCoopers LLP
REPRONIG	Reproduction Right Society of Nigeria
SACD	Société des Auteurs et Compositeurs Dramatiques
SACEM	Société des Auteurs, Compositeurs et Editeurs de Musique
SAMRO	Southern African Music Rights Organisation
SARRAL	South African Recording Association Limited
TRIPS	Trade Related Aspects of Intellectual Property
UOLTJ	University of Ottawa Law and Technology Journal
UN	United Nations
UN Charter	Universal Declaration of Human Rights
UNESCO	United Nations Education Scientific and Cultural Organisation
WASP	Wireless Application Service Providers Association of Nigeria Ltd/Gte
WCT	WIPO Copyright Treaty
WIPO	World Intellectual Property Organisation
WPPT	WIPO Performances and Phonograms Treaty

Chapter 1
Introduction

1.1 Structure and Brief Overview of Chapters

This work is divided into five chapters. The first is the Introduction discussing the link between Copyright and creativity and how from the beginning, creativity has played a pivotal role in development. The issue of balancing the interest of the author and user is also highlighted, and lastly the concept of Collective Administration of Copyright and Related Rights, its role and justification, is explored.

The second chapter will trace the evolution of Collective Administration in Nigeria. It will trace generally the history of Copyright and create a link to Collective Administration, as well as addressing how the evolution of Collective Administration in Nigeria fits into this.

The third chapter will discuss the legal framework for collective administration in Nigeria and will, in this regard, examine the pre-independence and post-independence legislation as well as past and the existing regulations issued by appropriate authorities dealing with the regulation and administration of Copyright Collective Management Organizations.

The fourth chapter deals with the regulatory challenges in the administration of Copyright in Nigeria, and will attempt to identify the problems encountered with Collective Management Organizations in Nigeria, the steps taken so far to address them, the role of the courts as well as legislative reforms.

The concluding chapter will consider the way forward and will attempt a comparative analysis between the collective management regulatory regimes of South Africa and Nigeria, with the aim of extracting lessons for the future.

O. Ola, *Copyright Collective Administration in Nigeria*, SpringerBriefs in Law,
DOI: 10.1007/978-3-642-35819-7_1, © The Author(s) 2013

1.2 Background

1.2.1 Creativity at the Beginning

In the beginning, God created the heavens and the earth.[1] In the process we are told of the making of two great lights, one to rule the day and the other the night and to serve as signs for seasons, days, and years.[2] These two great lights are then set in the heavens to give light upon earth. My reading of the account of this story makes me ponder on the role of creativity to development. The story shows how creativity was active at the beginning of times and shaped the coming into existence of the heavens and earth and all that moves and thrives within them. The Creator[3] demonstrates the ability of creating "something out of nothing", as exemplified in the creation of man; and further "something out of something", as perhaps exemplified in the Bible story of Noah's making of an ark,[4] there by laying out the model and essence of creativity.

In the case of the making of the ark, which was supposedly the first of its kind, it is interesting to note that the ark was made of gopher wood[5] (something that already existed) *with the intent of saving the world from an impending flood* (i.e., the greater good).[6] Thus, the model and essence of creativity referred to above encapsulates the doctrine of the public interest, as aptly captured in the opening statement of the final report on limitations and exceptions to Copyright: 'It is a well-established principle of Copyright doctrine that the qualified grant of proprietary rights over the fruits of creative enterprise is directed first and foremost at the promotion of the public interest'.[7] The making of an aircraft by the Wright Brothers in the early 1900s is another picture of the "something out of nothing"

---

[1] This is the creation story found in the Holy Bible, Book of Genesis, Chapter 1, where, in creating the heavens and the earth, God is said to have made the light, firmament, sun, moon, stars, plants, animals and finally man.

[2] The Holy Bible *King James Version* Genesis Ch1 V:16–17.

[3] I am aware that there are different schools of thought on the beginning and the origin of man. This paper is however, not focused on the issue of the origin of man or the beginning of time. The focus is on the role of creativity as enunciated by the authors of the Holy Bible.

[4] See The Holy Bible *King James Version* Genesis 6:14–22 where at v.14 it says "make thee an ark of gopher wood; rooms shalt thou make in the ark, and shalt pitch it within and without with pitch".

[5] Ibid.

[6] The Holy Bible *King James Version* Genesis 6:17.

[7] Hugenholtz and Okediji *Limitation and Exceptions* 6.

and "something out of something" concept.[8] Although the principles of aerodynamics had existed prior to the works of the Wright Brothers,[9] it was their dogged exercise of their creative faculties that brought in this new invention with the aid of knowledge that had already existed.[10]

The creation of the heavens and the earth, the sun, the moon, the stars, their placement in the firmament, the creation of plants, and finally man as well as the invention of the Wright Brothers appear to have been equally designed to bring development to humanity.[11] The making of man from dust can be likened to the work of a sculptor who out of dust, clay, or other materials makes images. The dynamic make up of man, his brain with its several numbered cells, the focus of the eyes, the positioning of the nose, the functions of the mouth, the operations of the heart, the flow of blood, the complexity in the reproductive system of the female human being, the twin kidney positioning and functions, as well as several other components in the make-up of man tells that sufficient effort by all standards had been expended on the work and in putting together what today is called the human being.

From the story, the originality of the product called man is not in question. He had never existed; he was a pure product of creative imagination. In line with this thinking, it could for a moment be suggested that man himself is in the nature of a Copyright work. Works eligible for Copyright under Nigerian Copyright law[12] include artistic works.[13] The art of making a thing from dust falls most probably

---

[8] In Answers in genesis available online at http://www.answersingenesis.org/articles/cm/v13/n4/wright, *Date of use*: 14 May 2012 the belief by the Wright Brothers in the creation story has being attributed as their inspiration for the making of the first airplane. It was noted that "From studying God's creation in the form of bird-flight, they were helped to develop their own creation of a better aircraft". Of course, I am aware of the fact that the intellectual property right involved in the case of the Wright Brothers was patents rights rather than copyright. I am however, at this stage, concerned with highlighting the creative process and the idea of the public interest, which is the same with regard to all forms of intellectual property rights.

[9] See http://www.notablebiographies.com/We-Z/Wright-Brothers.html#b *Date of use*: 29 April 2012 where it was noted that "[t]he exploits of one of the great glider pilots of the late nineteenth century, Otto Lilienthal, had attracted the attention of the Wright Brothers as early as 1891, but it was not until the death of this famous aeronautical (having to do with the study of flying and the design of flying machines) engineer in 1896 that the two became interested in gliding experiments. They then decided to educate themselves in the theory and state of the art of flying".

[10] See ibid where it was noted that "The first flight was made by Orville and lasted only 12 s, during which the airplane flew 120 ft. That same day, however, on its fourth flight, with Wilbur at the controls, the plane stayed in the air for 59 s and traveled 852 ft. Then a gust of wind severely damaged the craft. The brothers returned to Dayton convinced of their success and determined to build another machine. In 1905, they abandoned their other activities and concentrated on the development of aviation. On 22 May 1906, they received a patent for their flying machine".

[11] See The Holy Bible *King James Version* Genesis 1:14–18 where the intent and purposes for the firmament, sun moon and stars was clearly spelt out. "And God said let there be lights in the firmament of the heaven to divide the day from the night; and let them be for signs, and for seasons, and for days, and years; and let them be for lights…to give light upon the earth".

[12] The Nigerian Copyright Act, Cap C28 Laws of the Federation of Nigeria 2004 (hereinafter referred to as the Nigerian Copyright Act).

[13] Section 1(1) c Nigerian Copyright Act.

within the category of artistic works and more particularly within the sphere of a work of sculpture.[14] The process of the making of man, as outlined in the Bible, would conform squarely to the process of the making of a sculpture, thus prompting the classification of man as an artistic work protectable by some celestial Copyright law. The argument may thus be put forward that if the making of man could be likened to the making of a sculpture, by any stretch of imagination, man could then himself be considered a Copyright or Copyrightable work.

Let us agree that the author was in the mountaintop of some mythical experience. Having come out of the trance and into the world of reality, the fact, however, remains that the idea behind the recognition of the creative effort of an original creator, that is, the encouragement of distinct thought processes and the venture to do what has not been done, through the sheer genius of individual "symbolic expressions",[15] is something clearly held in great esteem by most of humanity, stemming from the fact that creativity engenders development and the fact that Copyright remains the bedrock of creativity.[16]

Nevertheless, although we can argue that creativity was present at the very beginning, we cannot say the same for Copyright. The modern concept of "Copyright" was first introduced by the statute of Anne,[17] which vested property rights in creative works, particularly printed books and other writings, in the creator. In addition to this right, the author was also given the exclusive right to exploit the work for 21 years in respect of published books and 14 years for those books composed but not yet printed or published. The history of Copyright will be discussed in Chap. 2.

1.2.2 Exploring Copyright

Copyright can be described as the exclusive right of the owner of Copyright to control the exploitation of his work and to grant authorization to others in this regard, subject to certain limitations and exceptions.[18] The administration of Copyright is governed by International and national legal frameworks;

---

[14] Section 51 of the Nigerian Copyright Act provides that artistic works include irrespective of artistic quality, works of sculpture.

[15] See Mihaly 1997 NAMTA (22) 60, who expounding on "flow and creativity" noted that the poets and artists in the times of Michelangelo were considered individuals who could provide new symbolic expressions or could think differently from others. In other words, these individuals were considered creative.

[16] See in this regard the response of the publishing industry to the Hargreaves report. http://copyright-debate.co.uk/?p=667 *Date of use*: 14 March 2012.

[17] 8, Anne C. 19.

[18] See Fitzgerald et al. *Oak Law Project Report* 21; where Copyright was defined as a type of intellectual property founded on a person's creative skill and labor. It allows the copyright owner to control acts (such as copying) and to prevent others from using protected materials without permission, unless an exception applies.

International in the sense that several International instruments such as the Berne convention,[19] Universal Copyright Convention,[20] Rome Convention,[21] WIPO Copyright Treaty,[22] WIPO Performance and Phonograms Treaty,[23] Geneva Phonograms Convention[24] and the Agreement on Trade Related Aspects of Intellectual Properties (WTO-TRIPS)[25] contain provisions relating to the international and national administration of Copyright and related rights. This they do by recognizing the sovereignty of each member nation and allowing the national legislation of these countries to determine issues that are considered domestic or peculiar to each nation and that may affect the nation's sovereignty.

Copyright controls the grant of rights in respect of certain 'works'—works such as literary works, artistic works, musical works, sound recordings, cinematograph films, and broadcasts.[26] Interestingly, except for program-carrying signals, published editions and computer programs, which are provided for in the South African Copyright Act,[27] the Copyright Acts of both Nigeria and South Africa cover the exact same works and use the same language in this regard. The United States Copyright Act[28] in specifying the subject matter of Copyright provides for works similar to those listed in the Nigerian and South African Copyright Act's but extends its subject matter of works to include "pantomimes and choreographic works; pictorial, graphic, sculptural works and architectural works".[29] It should be noted that some of these additional works referred to herein, although not protected as distinct works, are also covered by the Nigerian and South African Copyright Acts under certain categories of works; for instance, sculptures and architectural works are covered under artistic works as provided at Section 1(1) iii of the South African Copyright Act and at Section 51(1) of the Nigerian Copyright Act, while choreography is covered under dramatic works at Section 1(1) xix of the South

---

[19] Berne Convention for the Protection of Literary and Artistic Works 1971. (Hereinafter referred to as **Berne Convention**). The initial act was passed in 1886 and has been revised/amended five times namely at Berlin 1908, Rome 1928, Brussels 1948, Stockholm 1967, and Paris 1971 but further amended in 1979.

[20] Universal Copyright Convention 1952.

[21] Rome convention, 1961 International Convention for the Protection of Performers, Producers of Phonograms and Broadcasting Organisations done at Rome on 26 October 1961.

[22] Adopted in Geneva on 20 December 1996 (Hereinafter referred to as WCT).

[23] Adopted in Geneva on 20 December 1996 (Hereinafter referred to as WPPT).

[24] Convention for the Protection of Producers of Phonograms against Unauthorized Duplication of their Phonograms of 29 October 1971. The agreement was passed based on concerns at the widespread and increasing unauthorized duplication of phonograms and the damage occasioned to the interests of authors, performers and producers of phonograms.

[25] Annex 1c to the agreement establishing the World Trade Organization.

[26] Section 1(1) a–f, Nigerian Copyright Act.

[27] Section 2(1) of the South African Copyright Act, No 98 of 1978 (Hereinafter referred to as the Copyright Act of 1978).

[28] Copyright Act of 1976, Pub. L. No. 94–553, 90 Stat. 2541 (title 17 of the *United States Code*, 19 October 1976 (Hereinafter referred to as the United States Copyright Act).

[29] Section 102 United States Copyright Act.

African Copyright Act. The wordings of some other works are also couched differently; for instance, it talks of motion pictures and other audiovisual works while the Nigerian and South African Copyright Acts capture these as cinematograph films.[30] The underpinning of this is that new forms of works are created as technology advances, and these products of creativity continue to enrich humanity. As stated in the Preamble to the United States Copyright Act, the protection of the works is aimed at promoting the progress of Science and Useful Arts.

Hundreds of years before this, when the first Copyright Act was passed, the Preamble to that Act aptly captured the intentions of the Act as "an act for the encouragement of learning… and for the encouragement of learned men to compose and write useful books".[31] In this regard this statute had a dual focal objective: first a user-focused objective, namely the encouragement of learning; and second, an author-focused objective, namely the encouragement of creativity. The Act thus sought to strike a balance between the interest of the authors and that of users.[32] Around 1709 when the Statute was passed, it appears that there was a practice of using or should one say exploiting printed and written works of authors without their consent.[33] Victor Hugo, in the 1870s, as chair of l'Association Littéraire Internationale opining on the subject noted that

> Before the publication, the author has an undeniable and unlimited right. Think of a man like Dante, Molière, Shakespeare. Imagine him at the time when he has just finished a great work. His manuscript is there, in front of him; suppose that he gets the idea to throw it into the fire; nobody can stop him. Shakespeare can destroy Hamlet, Molière Tartufe, Dante the Hell.
>
> But as soon as the work is published, the author is not any more the master. It is then that other persons seize it: call them what you will: human spirit, public domain, society. It is such persons who say: I am here; I take this work, I do with it what I believe I have to do, […] I possess it, it is with me from now on…[34]

The implication was that authors were deprived of a means of earning and livelihood generated through their written and now-printed materials.[35] It is no

[30] See Section 1(1) viii of the Copyright Act of 1978 and Section 51(1) of the Nigerian Copyright Act.

[31] Statute of Anne, (8 Anne C. 19). This statute is usually quoted to have been enacted in 1709 but a careful reading of the statute indicates that it was passed in 1710.

[32] See Gervais *Making Copyright Whole* 2008 5:1 & 2 UOLTJ 1 where he noted that "The time has come to make copyright whole… and to recognize that both authors and users require a functioning copyright system".

[33] Roger *The Changing Role of Copyright* http://copyright-debate.co.uk/?p=159 *Date of use*: 14 March 2012.

[34] http://www.copyrighthistory.com/quotations.html; (*Date of use*: 8 March 2012).

[35] Iain Stevenson *Why Copyright is still important after 300 years*: http://copyright-debate.co.uk/?p=424: *Date of use*: 14 March 2012.

wonder then that agitations for the enactment of the Statute of Anne were well pronounced.[36] In its opening recitals, the statute stated

> printers, booksellers and other persons have of late frequently taken the liberty of printing, reprinting and publishing or causing to be printed, reprinted, and published, books and other writings, without the consent of the authors or proprietors of such books and writings, to their very great detriment, and too often to the ruin of them and their families: for preventing therefore such practices for the future…[37]

One cardinal message from the words of Victor Hugo and the Statute of Anne is the fact that creative works are capable of being exploited whenever men have access to them and believe that such works are useful. The unfortunate part of this is that the exploitation is often carried out without the consent of the authors or proprietors, which brings about very detrimental effects to the authors or owners, as the case may be. To prevent the practice of use without consent and to ameliorate the detrimental effects on authors and owners, it became necessary to put protections in place.[38] Over the years, these protections have grown and indeed increased.[39] However, the granting of protection does not, in itself, address a cardinal question, namely: How do people desirous of using or exploiting useful books, music, artistic works or other works in which Copyright subsist obtain consent to use such works? This question is germane seeing that the author of a useful book may be located in Cape Town, South Africa while an interested user is located in Abuja, Nigeria.

The challenges of distance, means of communication, ability to actually locate the author, and response time by the author to the intended user are all issues for consideration. While considering the aforementioned issues, it is also pertinent to note that these issues are of concern in respect of virtually all categories of works, and even more so in the modern day and not only in respect of literary works as was the case in 1710. Therefore, moving away from the 1710s into the present age, we are often confronted with a situation where a particular work can be a combination of several works holding multiple rights,[40] and therefore requiring several

[36] Ibid.

[37] 8 Anne C 19.

[38] The Statute of Anne gave sole right and liberty for 21 years to authors of books already published and for books composed but not yet printed or published; 14 years sole right and liberty to print and reprint was given.

[39] Today, the term of protection for copyright has increased with the Berne Convention providing at Article 7(1) for the minimum term of protection for the life of the author plus 50 years after his death. Most countries like Nigeria have gone in excess of 50 years term of protection provided in the Berne Convention and now provide for the life of the author plus 70 years after his death.2q.

[40] A music CD for instance, is a combination of several works including lyrics (a literary work), musical notes (musical work), the performance of the lyrics and musical notes, and the sound recording of the performance. This single work consisting several works holds several potentials: for instance it could be broadcast on television or satellite (rights of broadcast, communication to the public, viewing at a place and time of ones choice), it could be played at a public place such as a hotel or bar (public performance), it could be translated from one language to another

consents from the various authors and owners of each work before a user can have legitimate use of such work(s).

Thus the question posed above, namely how users are to obtain the requisite consent from the varied authors and owners of works and rights, taking cognizance of the challenges that may be posed by time, location, cost and several other considerations, and yearns for an answer. It is strongly suggested that one effective response to these questions is the utilization of the system of collective administration of Copyright.

1.3 Statement of the Problem

1.3.1 Collective Management of Copyright and Related Rights

Collective Management of Copyright and its related rights is a system in which "owners of rights authorize Collective Management Organizations to monitor the use of their works, negotiate with prospective users, give them licenses against appropriate remunerations on the basis of a tariff system and under appropriate conditions, collect such remuneration and distribute it among the owners of rights".[41] The rationale for this system of management arises from the impracticability of managing these activities individually,[42] namely the inability of the individual right owner to personally monitor and enforce all of his rights in every situation where his works are used.[43] This system enables right owners inclusive of Nigerian authors such as D'banj, Tu Face Idibia, Tosin Martin and a host of others, to concentrate on creativity while leaving the management of their rights to those who are best suited for doing so,[44] while also giving an assurance that reward for creativity will accrue to the right owners through payment of royalties as and when due. The benefit of the system is also double edged, in the sense that not only does it safeguard the interests of authors, but it also provides an accessible and easy-to-

(Footnote 40 continued)
(translation), it could be reproduced and sold (reproduction and distribution), the sales could be structured as hard copy sales and online sales and a video of the work could be built or part of it incorporated in a cinematograph film (making a cinematograph film of the work and synchronization). All of these usages are covered by different rights making the use of the singular work subject to multiple rights.

[41] Fiscor *Collective Management of Copyright and Related Rights* 17.

[42] http://www.wipo.int/about-ip/en/about_collective_mngt.html (*Date of use*: 6 March 2012).

[43] Adewopo *Nigerian Copyright Systems Principles and Perspectives* 81.

[44] In this regard, Gervais 2011 COLUM-VLA J.L. & ARTS 427 notes that "It is also in the nature of CMO's that rights management is not incidental to their work..., Rights management is what CMO's do".

use platform to users desirous of engaging in legitimate exploitation of a work.[45] Thus, collective management serves the purpose of bridging the gap between owners and users by simultaneously addressing the needs and concerns of both parties under a single platform.

1.3.2 Authors' Rights and Collective Management of Rights'

Authors' wear several caps depending on the work in contemplation. The Nigerian Copyright system covers six broad categories of works as follows: literary, artistic, musical, cinematograph film, sound recording, and broadcasting.[46] The South African Copyright system provides for the six works mentioned in the Nigerian Copyright act and goes even further to provide for program carrying signals, published editions and computer programs.[47] The creation of these works is attributable to the *author*—and the interpretation section of the South African Copyright Act as well as that of the Nigerian Act, provides among other things for the definition of an author and specifically provides in respect of Musical, Literary, and Artistic works that the author is the person who first created the work.[48] On the other hand, the author of a sound recording is the person by whom arrangements for making the recording was made. In all of these, whatever work is used is a work in which the author has rights, rights which oftentimes are bundled, that is, the work holds several rights simultaneously, as elaborated upon below.

Rights that accrue to the author have been clearly spelt out in several international conventions and national legislations and include rights of reproduction,[49] performance,[50] making available,[51] communication to the public,[52] broadcast,[53]

[45] Fiscor *Collective Management of Copyright and Related Rights* 16.

[46] Section 1(1) a–f, Nigerian Copyright Act Cap C28 2004 (Hereinafter referred to as the Nigerian Copyright Act).

[47] Section 2(1) South African Copyright Act No 98 of 1978, as amended (hereinafter referred to as the South African Copyright Act).

[48] In respect of photographs, the South African and Nigerian definition of an author is the Person Responsible for its composition and the person who took the photograph, respectively.

[49] Article 9 Berne Convention, Articles 7 & 11 WPPT. While Art 7 provides for right of performers, Art 11 provides for Right of Producers of Phonogram Section 6(1)(a)I, 6(1)(b)1, 6(1)(c)1 and 7(1) a of the Nigerian Copyright Act in respect of Literary and Musical, Artistic, Cinematograph and Sound recording respectively and Sections 6, 7 & 8 South African Copyright Act in respect of Literary and Musical, Artistic and Cinematograph film respectively.

[50] Article 14(1)ii, Berne Convention (particularly in respect of Literary and Artistic works).

[51] Articles 10 & 14 WPPT for Performers in respect of fixed performances and producers of phonogram in respect of their phonograms; Art 8 WCT.

[52] Articles 11bis (i, ii & iii) and 14(1)ii Berne Convention; Article 8 WCT,

[53] Article 11bis Berne Convention; Article 15 WPPT.

rental,[54] distribution,[55] adaptation,[56] and translation".[57] The nature of these rights is such that their management and enforcement is practically beyond the capacity of any individual right owner. Having indicated this, it has to be mentioned that not all the rights listed above would be difficult to exercise by individual right owners—indeed some of the rights are such that the users' demand for such rights is very low, and hence the need for collective management of such rights may not be necessary.[58] Thus works such as musical comedies, operas, operetta, and ballets (so-called grand right works)[59] are usually exclusively licensed by the individual Copyright owner, rather than through a collecting society. The staging of an opera or other performances of dramatic-musical works is not an activity that occurs as often as the playing of music or other non-dramatic works in a hotel, hence while the performance of music or the communication to the public of a recorded music performance in a hotel, bar, restaurant, or other public places is usually covered under the purview of the collective management structure, the use of the performances of a dramatic-musical work in an opera is nevertheless usually licensed individually, as a grand rights work, since such performances do not occur very frequently (and where they do, individual monitoring of such use can easily be done by right owners).[60]

The role of collective management is thus most prominent when it comes to the use of the rights of public performance,[61] broadcast and reproduction. The rights of public performance and broadcast are generally administered by what are called 'performing rights societies' while the rights of reproduction are administered by 'mechanical rights societies'.[62] The right of making available has now come to prominence with the advent of digital technology through transmission by wire or wireless means, enabling users to access content at a time and place of their choice. This notwithstanding, it has been said that "... the activities of authors'

---

[54] Articles 9 & 13 WPPT.

[55] Articles 8 & 12 WPPT.

[56] Article 12 Berne Convention.

[57] Article 8 Berne Convention.

[58] Fiscor *Collective Management of Copyright and Related Rights* 38.

[59] See in relation to grand rights http://www.unimelb.edu.au/copyright/information/music-licence.html (*Date of use*: 10 March 2012). Where it is indicated that **grand right works** also known as **grand right performances** are works where the performance of a Musical work is combined with a dramatic performance, (dramatic musical work). They include musical comedy, oratorio, choral work, opera, play with music, revue or ballet. In the United States for example, the principal Performing Rights Societies, Association of Composers Authors and Publishers (ASCAP) Broadcast Music Inc (BMI) and SESAC do not license dramatic performance rights. However, SACD in France and a few other collecting societies in other territories licenses grand rights.

[60] Kendrick *Grand Performing Right* 12.

[61] The right of public performance is also referred to as **small rights**. Small rights refer to performing rights in respect of "certain rights in certain categories of musical works" (see Fiscor *Copyright Management of Copyright and Related Rights* 37).

[62] Although in several instances one society may administer both *performing* and *mechanical* rights.

performing rights societies still represent the fullest system of…collective-management of rights".[63]

A musician who has written, performed, and recorded a song may have his song played on several radio and television stations across the 36 states of Nigeria and beyond. Works of music and video are often publicly performed and communicated to varied publics on aircrafts, buses, hotels, and several other public places both locally and internationally. Ordinarily, prior to the communication to the public or other kinds of use, of an author's work, requisite negotiation, and licensing (i.e., authorization) ought to take place. However, this authorization is often not obtained and in practical terms it may not be quite feasible for the author to go to all radio and television stations within and outside Nigeria to monitor and enforce use of the work. It is also impracticable for an individual to monitor all use, as the scope of use is clearly beyond the capacity of an individual. It is this impracticability and lack of ability of the right owner to adequately administer and protect his Copyright that has necessitated the rise of collective agencies or societies that would stand in the gap between right owners and users.[64]

1.3.3 Regulation of Collective Management Organizations in Nigeria

The regulatory and operational framework for collective administration in Nigeria is as provided for under the Nigerian Copyright Act[65] and the Copyright (Collective Management Organization) Regulation.[66] The Copyright Act of Nigeria has been amended twice. The first amendment of the Act, done in 1992, among other things introduced regulatory provisions to collective administration,[67] and a further amendment was done in 1999 empowering the Commission to carry out enforcement activities.[68]

Section 39 of the Copyright Act 2004 provides at subsection 1 as follows:

> A Collecting Society (in this section referred to as "a society") may be formed in respect of anyone or more rights of Copyrights owners for the benefit of such owners, and the society may apply to the Commission for approval to operate as a collecting society for the purpose of this Act.

---

[63] See *Fiscor Copyright Management of Copyright and Related Rights* 37.

[64] At http://www.wipo.int/edocs/mdocs/enforcement/en/acmc_1/acmc_1_1-main1.pdf. (*Date of use*: 13 March 2012) Gervais noted that "CMO's try to make copyright compliance as easy as possible".

[65] Section 39 Nigerian Copyright Act.

[66] The regulation was issued and published in the Official Gazette pursuant to the approval of the Honorable Attorney General of the Federation and Minister for Justice on 3 October 2007 as No. 98 of Volume 94.

[67] Sections 17 & 39 Nigerian Copyright Act.

[68] See Section 37 Nigerian Copyright Act.

It further provides at subsection (4) that

> It shall be unlawful for any group of persons to purport to perform the duties of a society without the approval of the Commission as required under this section of this Act.

The combined effect of these provisions is that the approval by the Nigerian Copyright Commission is a prerequisite to the operation of any society performing or desirous of performing the functions of a collecting society.

The rationale for this has been that the monopolistic nature of collecting societies requires some level of governmental control, more importantly because the state is obliged to deter anti-trust activities. This reasoning is even more pressing in Nigeria's setting, being a developing nation where anti-trust laws[69] are not adequately captured with regard to the operation and activities of collective management organizations in comparison to other organisations involved in trading and other economic activities.[70]

This work, therefore, analyzes the operation and regulation of Copyright Collective Management Organizations in Nigeria and discusses on whether or not the current operational and regulatory framework is best suited for the Nigerian creative industry. Answer to these questions would be proffered by tracing the evolution of collective administration in Nigeria and reviewing the experiences so far on collective administration in Nigeria, with the hope to show that while a regulatory framework for collective administration in Nigeria is crucial and thus welcome, balance is required. The aim would also be to expound on the possibility of the government allowing the private sector to steer its own ship in this area, taking cognizance of the fact that overregulation could stifle development.

The significance of this work lies in the possibility of exploring, identifying, and proffering suggested solutions to the causes of the challenges in collective administration in Nigeria against the back drop of the recurring problems that have ensued in the collective administration of Copyright and Related Rights in Nigeria. The Commission and indeed the entire Copyright sector have been enmeshed in the battle of *a regulated against a non-regulated* collective administration sector for about 20 years. The frustration of right owners can best be described as unbearable, because the embattled sector appears to have debarred right owners the fruit of their labor, as the societies are constantly involved in litigations and rarely pay royalties to authors, thus unable to focus on the essence of their existence.[71] The numerous problems and legal battles referred to herein ostensibly arise from the introduction of a regulatory framework in the area of collective management of rights.

---

69 Gervais COLUM-VLA J.L. & ARTS 436.

70 See generally, Adewopo, *Nigerian Copyright System: Principles and Perspectives* 88–89.

71 See generally Okoroji *Copyright Neighboring Rights & the New Millionaires* 206.

Chapter 2
Tracing the Evolution of Collective Management Organisations in Nigeria

2.1 Introduction

This chapter seeks to trace the evolution of the concept of collective management as a phenomenon in copyright history and how it became an established norm in many jurisdictions today as a part and parcel of copyright administration and practice. It then examines the Nigerian history of collective administration which has become a notorious feature of its copyright system.

Tracing the evolution of Collective Management Organisations in Nigeria is akin to a man tracing his linage. There is a main source, the beginning point from which it all grows out and the pattern appears coherent till a point where it begins to grow branches which in themselves grow other branches, and the process simply replicates itself with an intrinsic trait in each branch to be systematically traced back to the origin. This chapter wishes to trace a specific genealogical evolution, namely that of Nigeria's Copyright Collective Management Organizations.

2.2 The Origin

The evolutionary origin can be traced back to about 1777[1] and more specifically to the 3rd of July 1777, when Beaumarchais[2] gathered 22 authors, some of the most influential creative writers at that time.[3] This gathering appears to have arisen from a complaint lodged by Beaumarchais expressing his displeasure regarding the remuneration from Comédie Française in respect of performances of his "Barbier de Séville". In the writing, "A Field of Honor: Intermission",[4] it was noted as follows:

---

1 http://www.gutenberg-e.org/brg01/print/brg05.pdf *Date of use*: 17 March 2012.

2 Ibid. Pierre Augustin Caron de Beaumarchais was his full name.

3 See http://www.gutenberg-e.org/brg01/print/brg05.pdf *Date of use*: 17 March 2012 where it was noted that prior to the actions of Beaumarchais, Lonvay, Mercier, and Palissot had brought lawsuits whilst Cailhava, Renou, and Rutlidge, printed the grievances, and challenges they had against the royal theater. These men were also writers and contemporaries of Beaumarchais.

4 Anon *A Field of Honor: Intermission* Available on line at http://www.gutenberg-e.org/brg01/print/brg05.pdf *Date of use*: 17 March 2012.

DOI: 10.1007/978-3-642-35819-7_2,

> After years of delay, it had been first performed on February 23, 1775, and then substantially revised, before beginning a hugely successful run. By the end of 1776, it had been performed profitably 32 times and had generated a gross receipt of more than 93,000. However, when the troupe leaders wrote him, they did not use the respectful and courteous tone evident in their correspondence with established writers; instead, they violated royal regulations by asking Beaumarchais to 'make arrangements with us to lose your share of the proceeds from the work, but at least,... have the pleasure of seeing your play performed more often'.

Prior to the complaint lodged by Beaumarchais, other writers whose works had been performed and were dissatisfied had also made similar complaints, but they all fell on deaf ears.[5] Beaumarchais's complaint could however not be ignored as he was a person of influence. In this regard it was noted of Beaumarchais that.

> He possessed a combination of various forms of cultural capital that Lonvay, Mercier, and the others had not. Foremost, Beaumarchais was politically well-connected. The Minister of the Royal Household, Antoine Jean Amelot de Chaillou, and the Duke de Duras, one of the First Gentlemen, both instructed the troupe leaders to meet with Beaumarchais. Indeed, these courtiers and the Comédiens knew him to be a protégé of the Count de Maurepas, first minister to the newly ascendant Louis XVI. Thus Beaumarchais carried greater political weight than other playwrights who had previously negotiated with and even sued the Comédie Française. The Comédiens were therefore less certain of having a potential lawsuit by Beaumarchais dismissed from the courts.
>
> Secondly, they knew that Beaumarchais had already demonstrated himself an able propagandist and astute manipulator of public opinion in his printed Mémoires contre Goezmann in the early 1770s.[6]

It was this peculiar influence which Beaumarchais had acquired that prompted the comedians[7] to heed his complaint and enter negotiations with him, thereby suggesting a review of the Royal Theatre Regulation. It was in response to this that Beaumarchais invited twenty-two author playwrights to his residence at the corner of the rue vieille du Temple and the rue des Blancs Monteaux.[8] The meeting, which was held on the 3rd of July 1777 could be regarded as the birth of the first collective management organization, Société des Auteurs et Compositeurs Dramatiques (SACD),[9] a professional association for creative writers domiciled in France.

---

[5] Ibid.

[6] Anon *A Field of Honor: Intermission*', Ibid.

[7] Ibid at page 2. Duke de Duras was the First Gentleman primarily responsible for overseeing the Comédie Française in 1777. He decided to use Beaumarchais's complaint as an opportunity to revise the royal theater regulations. He thus wrote to Beaumarchais on the 15th of June 1777 requesting that he gather playwrights and other writers to express their opinions on how best to put an end to the incessant author-theater conflicts.

[8] Ibid at page 11. The house still stands in the Marais, and the doors still bear Beaumarchais's monogram.

[9] Anon "*Introduction to Collective Management of Copyright and Related Rights*" available online at http://uatm.com.ua/laws/int/Introduction%20to%20Collective%20Management%20of%20Copyright%20and%20Related%20Rights.pdf *Date of use*: 19 March 2012 noted that Société des auteurs et compositeurs dramatiques (SACD), was the first society dealing with the collective management of authors' rights.

Société des gens de lettres (SGDL) is said to have been the second collective management organization, in the field of literary works, and was constituted by French authors, amongst whom were notable names such as Honore' de Balzac, Alexandre Dumas, and Victor Hugo.[10] The first meeting of its general assembly is said to have been held at the end of 1837.[11] About 10 years after this (1847), "the concept of modern collective administration of copyright"[12] came to the fore through a legal action instituted by two composers Paul Henrion and Victor Parizot and a writer, Ernest Bourget, supported by their publisher, against "Ambassadeurs", a "café-concert" in the Avenue des Champs-Elysées in Paris. These gentlemen went to this café and whilst there, they heard the public performance of their work and pondered why they should pay any fees to the café for their seats and meals seeing that the café did not pay them for the exploitation of their work through public performance.[13] They, therefore, instituted an action in court to compel the café to pay them for the exploitation of their work. The court held in their favor and the café was obliged to pay a substantial amount of fees.[14] This decision opened a vista of opportunities for composers and text writers of non-dramatic musical works. It, however, soon became clear that the newly identified rights could not be administered effectively by individual rights holders, hence the formation in 1850 of what Adewopo has referred to as "the concept of modern collective administration of copyright"[15] a collecting agency which metamorphosized into the still-existing *Société des auteurs, compositeurs et éditeurs de musique* (SACEM).[16]

2.3 Transition

The late 1800s and early 1900s saw the formation of several collective management organizations, (particularly performing rights' societies) all around Europe and indeed other parts of the world.[17] In the wake of these formations, the Performing

---

[10] Fiscor *Collective Management of Copyright and Related Rights* 18.

[11] Ibid.

[12] Adewopo *Nigeria Copyright System* Principles and Perspectives 83.

[13] Fiscor Op cit (footnote 10).

[14] Fiscor *Collective Management of Copyright and Related Rights* 19.

[15] Adewopo Op cit (footnote 12).

[16] SACEM is still functioning till date.

[17] Performing rights societies are societies meant to represent owners of copyright in respect of their right to public performances of musical works. **Fiscor** noted in his work *Introduction to Collective Management of copyright and Related Rights* 6 that [t]he first full collective management systems...were established for the management of certain rights in certain categories of musical works. The musical works concerned were the so-called 'small rights' works and the rights involved were the so-called 'small rights' or, in other words, the so-called 'performing rights'. Small rights refer to those rights which are administered collectively, while grand rights are those generally administered individually. Some examples of performing rights

Right Society[18] (PRS) based in London, United Kingdom was established in 1914. The British Empire was at the time the largest empire in the world, controlling over a quarter of the Earth's land mass covering 33,700,000 km@\2 (13,012,000 sq mi), and boasted of over some 458 million people, which amounted to approximately one-fifth of the world's population at the time.[19] Nigeria was at the time a colony of the British Empire and by virtue of the reception[20] and application of English laws[21] which had been extended[22] to all British territories, Nigeria's Copyright System became governed by the recently passed Copyright Act of 1911.[23] It was shortly after the passage of this Act that the PRS[24] was formed to cater for the needs of right owners within the British Empire and as was the case with other countries under the British Administrative structure, the PRS became responsible for the collective administration of Copyright and related rights in Nigeria. At about 1940, royalties were paid by the old Nigerian Broadcast Service (NBS) to PRS for the use of music.[25] However after independence in 1960, and the subsequent enactment of the first indigenous Copyright Act in 1970,[26] which was also partly attributable to the need to build a strong political and economic structure free from colonial supervision,[27] the direct control and administration of Copyright and related rights by PRS had to give way to some other structure.

(Footnote 17 continued)
societies are the Performing Rights Society (PRS) 1914 (UK), The american society of composers authors and publishers (ASCAP) 1914 (USA), TONO 1928 (Norway), SESAC 1930 (USA), BMI 1939 (USA), SUISA 1942 (Switzerland).

18 See Okoroji *Copyright Neighbouring Rights and the New Millionaires* 189 where the organization was described as "one of the oldest and most successful collecting societies in the world". He noted further that "with respect to licensing of music for broadcasting and public performances within its territory, it is a virtual monopoly".

19 Ferguson, *Empire* 15.

20 See Park *The Sources of Nigerian Law* 15 where he opined that "the reception of laws, that is to say, the introduction into one territory of the legal rules of another, is a phenomenon by no means unique to the British possessions in Africa in the nineteenth century. There have in fact been many other examples, of which perhaps the best known is the reception in the Middle Ages of Roman law upon the continent of Europe".

21 Park supra at 93. The English Laws introduced into Nigeria comprised the Common law of England, Doctrine of Equity and Statues of General Application that were in force in England on the 1st day of January 1900.

22 By Order-in-Council No. 912 of 24th June 1912 The Copyright Act of 1911 was extended, in 1912, to the territory of Nigeria.

23 Copyright Act, 1911. [l & 2 GEO. 5. CH. 46.].

24 "The PRS is a company limited by Guarantee with no share capital and operating primarily in the U.K, but with agencies in countries of the Commonwealth where there are no indigenous collecting societies. Its membership consists of composers and publishers of musical works and the rights administered are essentially the public performing rights" See footnote 12.

25 Okoroji Op Cit (footnote 18).

26 Copyright Decree No. 61 of 1970.

27 Ndongko *Africa Spectrum* 53.

2.4 CMOs in Nigeria Become Indigenous

Shortly after the Nigerian civil war,[28] precisely in 1971, PRS was approached by a law firm in Nigeria[29] seeking to be appointed as its agent in Nigeria.

The first indigenous Copyright Act had been passed just a year before this and on the heels of the end of the war, there was the apparent need for the economy to be strategically refocused for national development. It is, therefore, not surprising why the law firm made such a request. The outcome of the request made to PRS by the law firm was aptly captured in the words of Okoroji when he said "Giwa and Atilade and Co who seemed to be the only Nigerian lawyers with any interest in the business of copyright, had little problem securing the PRS agency in the country".[30] Thus, the PRS-licensed agency Giwa and Atilade and Co could be regarded as the first indigenous organization to be responsible for collective administration of copyright and related rights in Nigeria. The agency had two major tasks to accomplish. The first was to get a good number of Nigerian composers to join the membership of PRS, and the second was to commence extensive licensing of users in Nigeria.[31] Considerable success was achieved on the first task with several popular names[32] joining the membership of PRS. The second task was vigorously pursued but despite the entreaties and efforts of Alhaji Giwa, most users simply refused to pay.[33] In fact the task was not accomplished.[34] In Okoroji's view, the lack of willingness to pay by users was based on the pretext that the number of Nigerians in the PRS membership was too small and that users would rather deal with a Nigerian institution.[35] To satisfy the aspiration of users who would rather deal with a Nigerian Institution, Alhaji Giwa set up the musical copyright society of Nigeria (MCSN), a company limited by guarantee, to administer the public performance right of musicians in Nigeria. The company was registered[36] on the 20 July 1984 and this marked the formation of the first full-fledged collective management organization in Nigeria.

---

[28] Also referred to as the "Nigerian-Biafran War" 6 July 1967–15 January 1970.

[29] The name of the Law firm was Giwa and Atilade and Co. It was a Lagos-based law firm with Fatai Oladele Giwa as the Principal partner of the firm.

[30] Okoroji *Copyright Neighbouring Rights and the New Millionaires* 192.

[31] Ibid.

[32] Ibid. The likes of Chief Ebenezer Obey, Victor Uwaifo, Rex Jim Lawson, Sonny Okosun, Sunny Ade and others were examples of Nigerian artist that joined the membership of PRS.

[33] Ibid.

[34] Okoroji Op cit (footnote 30).

[35] Ibid.

[36] Registration of companies is as provided under the Companies and Allied Matters Act (CAMA), Laws of the Federation of Nigeria 2004.

2.5 Musical Copyright Society of Nigeria

After the registration of Musical Copyright Society of Nigeria (MCSN), a contract of reciprocal representation was signed between PRS and MCSN in 1986 thereby terminating the earlier agency agreement between PRS and Giwa and Atilade and Co.[37] MCSN exists to the present day but not without several challenges. (These challenges shall be discussed in the next chapter in depth.)

The formation and subsequent operations of MCSN apparently did not satisfy the yearnings of all right owners in the music industry and hence there was the clamor[38]

> For the establishment of a broad-based national collecting society that will provide opportunity for them to decide how their rights would be managed and to reflect the overall nationalistic aspirations of the creative community.[39]

2.6 Performing and Mechanical Rights Society of Nigeria (PMRS) and Copyright Society of Nigeria (COSON)

In response to the various agitations and taking advantage of the recently amended Nigerian Copyright Act[40] which now made provisions for the administration and regulation of collecting societies, a group of right owners consisting of performers, composers of music, and phonogram producers registered the Performing and Mechanical Rights Society of Nigeria (PMRS).[41] The organization was registered as a company limited by guarantee and upon request for approval to the Nigerian Copyright Commission; PMRS was approved,[42] marking the birth of the second collective management organization in Nigeria. Prior to this time, MCSN had applied[43] to the Nigerian Copyright Commission for approval to operate as a collecting society, in line with the Copyright (Amendment) Decree. The approval was, after due consideration, denied based on the refusal of MCSN to provide the

---

[37] Adewopo *Nigerian Copyright System Principles and Perspectives* 86.

[38] Okoroji Op Cit (footnote 30).

[39] Adewopo Op Cit (footnote 37) at 87.

[40] Copyright (Amendment) Decree No.98 of 1992. The amendments are now consolidated in Cap C28 of the Laws of the Federation of Nigeria, 2004.

[41] Okoroji Op cit (footnote 30) at 201 where he noted that "The many lessons learnt from several years of internal wrangling led to the adoption of the model which groups song writers, composers, publishers, performers and record producers in one collecting society.

[42] The said approval was given on the 22nd of December 1994. See Okoroji Op Cit (footnote 30) at 201.

[43] This application was dated the 25th of August 1993. See Okoroji Op Cit (footnote 30) at 200.

documents[44] requested by the Nigerian Copyright Commission and the fact that the structural composition of the organization did not represent a nationalistic interest, in view of the dominant position that the PRS and the Mechanical Copyright Protection Society (MCPS), both of the United Kingdom, had in MCSN. The Commission was consequently not convinced that the organization would cater for the interest of National creators.[45]

The combined effect of the denial of the application by MCSN for approval to function as a collecting society and the subsequent approval of PMRS was that the approval given PMRS had given it legal backing to operate as a collecting society, whilst the denial to MCSN had removed the legality behind a thriving structure. The reality was that PMRS neither had the infrastructure, nor the needed foreign co-operation[46] to enable it to negotiate reciprocal representation agreements.[47] Despite this shortcoming, the PMRS made efforts at issuing licenses locally,[48] but continued to struggle with regard to the licensing of international repertoire. MCSN, operating first as the "Giwa Agency" (and subsequently as MCSN after been duly registered), had already signed a reciprocal representation agreement[49] giving it the right to use PRS' repertoire in Nigeria. This situation resulted in MCSN becoming the de facto collecting society while PMRS was the de jure collecting society. It was, therefore, no surprise when agitations were made for the recognition of MCSN, especially to cater for the interest of its members, who were not represented, and were not willing to surrender their rights to PMRS, the approved society.

In its continued efforts to find a lasting solution to the agitations, and to liberalize collective administration, in May 2005 the Nigerian Copyright Commission granted approval to the MCSN to operate as a collecting society in

---

[44] Okoroji in his work opined that the documents which MCSN refused to provide were the membership and financial records of the organization. See Op Cit (footnote 30) at 200.

[45] The governing board of MCSN was comprised four members elected by the general meeting and four persons nominated by PRS and MCPS. Article 23(d) of the Articles of Association of the organization provided that "no resolution (at any general meeting) shall be deemed to have been carried, whether on a show of hands or on a poll, if the PRS or MCPS has voted against it".

[46] Okoroji Op cit (footnote 30) at 202.

[47] See Uchtenhagen *The Setting-up of New Copyright Societies* 19 where he noted the importance of new societies having the cooperation of foreign sister societies but also observed that "most established societies are not prepared to give "advance confidence" by the speedy signing of reciprocal agreement. They tend more to adopt the approach of entering into a contractual relationship only after the young copyright society has been accepted as a member of CISAC. However, CISAC makes conditional, understandably, on a degree of proven evidence, which in itself is very difficult to establish without demonstrated competence for managing the foreign repertoire".

[48] See Okoroji *Copyright, Neighbouring Rights and The New Millionaires* 201 where it was noted that the first ever license issued by PMRS was that issued to the organizers of a Benson and Hedges concert which held in Lagos on the 13th of December 1997.

[49] PRS_MCSN Contract of Reciprocal Representation Agreement signed on the 17th day of March 1986 in Lagos and on the 14th day of April 1986 in London. This agreement gave MCSN the right amongst other things to use the repertoire of PRS.

the music industry, alongside the existing PMRS. This action triggered a lot of protests from PMRS, who made representation to the government to withdraw the approval, leading to the subsequent withdrawal of the approval granted to the MCSN.[50] This generated a lot of controversy and eventually laid the ground for the reform of collective administration in Nigeria. The reform brought about the Copyright (collective management organization) Regulation 2007, in terms of which a call for applications from interested organizations to operate collective management organizations was made. Three applications were received in this respect for music and sound recording and after a thorough process the commission granted approval to the Copyright Society of Nigeria (COSON)[51] to cover the rights involving music and sound recording.

2.7 Repronig

The reach of collective administration in Nigeria spreads beyond just the music industry, covering also the literary sector. In this sector, right owners are represented by the Reproduction Right Society of Nigeria (REPRONIG).[52]

REPRONIG is a company limited by guarantee with its main object as negotiating and granting of licenses, as well as collecting, and distribution of royalties to right owners. It represents copyright owners in the literary sector and seeks to ensure that the reprographic rights of its members are protected and that members are adequately remunerated for the use of their works.

The organization was approved by the Nigerian Copyright Commission in 2001[53] and commenced operations on the 3rd of November 2003. Its approval has been renewed twice, first in 2004 and subsequently in 2007. It receives technical, financial, and international support for its operations from the Norwegian Reprographic Society, KOPINOR, who encouraged the formation of the society and has since inception supported its growth.[54] NORCODE is the agency that now plays the role of KOPINOR.[55] In recent times, REPRONIG has received indications from its development partners that the sponsorship it has so far enjoyed may

---

[50] See Adewopo *Nigerian Copyright System: Principles and Perspectives* 105; where it was noted that the Commission's decision elicited petitions from PMRS who sent a formal petition through the Honourable Minister of Culture and Tourism to the President. This petition led to a presidential directive withdrawing the approval granted to MCSN.

[51] PMRS vide a special resolution dated 29 September 2009 changed its name to COSON during the collective administration reform process.

[52] http://www.ifrro.org/members/reproduction-rights-society-nigeria *Date of use*: 21 March 2012 REPRONIG is a member of the international federation of reproduction rights organizations (IFRRO)

[53] Ibid. Where it indicated that REPRONIG was incorporated December 2000.

[54] Adewopo *Nigerian Copyright System Principles and Perspective* 88.

[55] http://www.norcode.no/en/links/ *Date of use*: 21st March 2012.

cease at any time. The reasons given were that it was expected that by now REPRONIG ought to be able to stand on its own and support itself.[56]

2.8 Tabulated Illustration

In a nutshell, the evolution of Copyright Collective Management Organizations can be traced in chronological order as seen from the tabulated diagram analyzed below (Table 2.1).

Table 2.1 Evolution of copyright collective management organizations

S/N	Name of organization	Name of prominent authors/facilitators	Year of formation	Comments
1.	Société des auteurs et compositeurs dramatiques (SACD)	Beaumarchais	1777	In France
2.	Société des gens de letters (SGDL)	1. Honore' de Balzac 2. Alexandre Dumas 3. Victor Hugo 4. and other French Writers	1837	In France
3.	Société des auteurs, compositeurs et éditeurs de musique (SACEM)	1. Paul Henriam 2. Victor Parizot 3. Ernest Bourget	1847	In France

In the late 1800s and early 1900s many collecting societies were formed all over Europe and other parts of the world. These include PRS (1914, UK), ASCAP (1914, USA), MCPS (1924, UK), TONO (1928, Norway), SESAC (1930, US), BMI (1939, US), SUISA (1942, Switzerland), SAMRO (1961, South Africa) etc. In Nigeria the evolution took the following form:

S/N	Name of organization	Name of prominent authors/facilitators	Year of formation	Comments
4.	Performing Rights Society (PRS)		1914	United Kingdom
5.	Giwa and Atilade and Co. (Giwa Agency)	Alhaji Giwa	1971	Nigeria
6.	Musical Copyright Society of Nigeria (MCSN)	Alhaji Giwa	1984	Nigeria
7.	Performing and Mechanical Rights Society of Nigeria (PMRS)	Tony Okoroji	1994	Nigeria
8.	Reproduction Rights Society of Nigeria (REPRONIG)	Dr Ekanem Inyang	2000	Nigeria
9.	Copyright Society of Nigeria (COSON)	Tony Okoroji	2010	Nigeria

[56] Op cit (footnote at 52).

Chapter 3
Legal Framework for Collective Management in Nigeria

3.1 Background

Every civilized society is made up of a system of rules, norms and laws that govern the activities of those living within it. The absence of such a system whether written or unwritten always results in anarchy[1] with everyone taking matters into his/her hands[2] and in the words of Eric Engle "leads straight to the law of the jungle with no exit".[3] A legal framework is that platform on which the what,[4]

---

[1] Engle 2008 35 N. Ky. L. Rev 1. Aristotle noted, that it is precisely the fact that humans live in States that marks human society and separates it from other social and specialized animals such as bees or wolves. Other animals are social. But human society is the most complex. Poetically, Aristotle notes that he who lives outside the state is either a brute beast or a god. Because humans are rational, political (social) animals with the gift of speech we live in cities and not as savages. Thus, our laws are higher than those of a dagger wielding thief.

[2] The Holy Bible, *King James Version* Judges 21:25. "In those days there was no king in Israel: every man did that which was right in his own eyes".

[3] Supra at footnote 1.

[4] See Carrol *Intellectual property rights* 15 where he addressed the "what" of a legal framework intertwining it with his heading by noting that "Intellectual property rights have been tailored before and will be tailored again". He further notes that "it is time to have a framework for analyzing this activity and to recognize its potential value in rendering intellectual property rights better suited to their task(s)".

O. Ola, *Copyright Collective Administration in Nigeria*, SpringerBriefs in Law,
DOI: 10.1007/978-3-642-35819-7_3, © The Author(s) 2013

why,[5] when,[6] and how[7] of a subject matter stands. It provides the rationale and justification[8] and the details of what should be done, why it should be done and the possible repercussions for failing to obey. As Litman[9] observed above, the practical relevance of a legal framework is not in its mere creation but in its acceptance and observance by the general public. Where the public is oblivious of the rules and even where they are aware but the laws do not conform to the deep-seated and generally-accepted norms and values of the general public, the outcome would be that the people would not accept, believe or obey such laws. Regardless of how laudable the goals, the rules are to achieve, the draftsmen of the law would need to go back to the drawing board, repeal the unacceptable ones, and put in place rules that are in tandem with the beliefs and acceptable values of the people.

3.2 Structures of Collective Management Organizations

The structural layout of Collective Management Organizations (CMO) differs from one organization to another and across countries.[10] These differences are usually influenced by the legislative framework under which each CMO operates.[11] These operating systems are numerous including the following:

---

[5] See Dinwoodie *One size fits all* 12 where he opined on "why" the Berne and Paris conventions were made noting that they were aimed at developing an international system designed to constrain rampant piracy and slowly expand core forms of protection.

[6] See Carrol Op cit (footnote 4) where he opines on "when and why" Intellectual property rights are granted. Answering from an economic point of view he notes that it stimulates investments in innovation and cultural productions.

[7] Ibid. In respect of the "how" Carrol noted that TRIPS followed the structural framework of minimum norms established by Berne and Paris. In his conclusion at page 14 he reasons that "clearly one size does not fit all" whether of a single Intellectual property regime or while still eradicating differences and applications of the rules within a single regime.

[8] See Litman *Copyright Non-Compliance* 427 where she discussed the dilemma of the user publics who generally do not believe that the laws that exist actually exist. She noted that "the trouble with the plan is that the only people who appear to actually believe that the current copyright rules apply as writ to every person on the planet are the member of the copyright bar… but that's a far cry from persuading the ten or twenty million new printers and reprinters".

[9] Ibid, Litman opined that "people don't obey laws that they don't believe in…Most people try to comply, at least substantially, with what they believe the law to say. If they don't believe the law says what it in fact says, though, they won't obey it-not because they are protesting its provisions, but because it doesn't stick in their heads".

[10] Gervais *Collective Management* 12 Available online at http://aix1.uottawa.ca/~dgervais/publications/collective_management.pdf.

[11] See the report Commissioned by the Copyright Licensing Agency and prepared by PricewaterhouseCoopers LLP (PwC) *"An economic analysis of copyright, secondary copyright, and collective licensing".* Available online at http://www.ipo.gov.uk/ipreview-c4e-sub-plsreport.pdf *Date of use: 24 March 2012 at 37.*

1. The legal basis on which the society operates[12]
2. The field of activity[13]
3. The ways rights are acquired[14]
4. Whether it is for-profit or not-for-profit[15]
5. The way they are managed (type of governance, type(s) of membership organization, agency, etc.);
6. The way they license (on a transactional basis, *i.e.*, work-by-work, or on a blanket or other basis); or
7. The way they distribute their funds (use of surveys, application of national treatment, use of funds for purposes other than distribution, etc.).

In a report produced by PricewaterhouseCoopers LLP (PwC),[16] considering among other things copyright collective management structures, reference was made to the International Federation of Reproduction Rights Organisation's (IFRRO) classification of the models of operation of collective management organizations as follows:

1. Voluntary collective licensing (e.g., US, Canada, UK) where organizations are free to license for reproduction rights either with an individual rights owner or a CMO mandated to act on the rights owners' behalf (but with no stipulation in law to govern this role).
2. Voluntary collective licensing with back-up in legislation which takes two forms:

a. Extended collective management (e.g., Norway). This follows the voluntary model above except that the agreements reached between users and CMOs are extended to cover rights owners who have not specifically mandated the CMO to act on their behalf. Rights owners are able to opt out of the CMO if they wish.

---

[12] Gervais Op cit footnote 10 where he identified the 4 main classifications under the Canadian Copyright law as follows:

1. Music performing and certain neighboring rights (Section 67 of the *Copyright Act*);
2. General regime (Section 70);
3. Particular cases" regime (retransmission and educational institutions Section 71); and
4. Private copying..

[13] Ibid. The Copyright Board listed existing Canadian collectives and identified the following areas:

1. Music
2. Literary
3. Audiovisual and multimedia
4. Visual arts
5. Retransmission
6. Private copying
7. Educational rights
8. Media monitoring.

[14] Ibid. Rights may be acquired voluntarily, non-voluntarily or by some other mechanism.

[15] See S.39 (2)a of the Nigerian Copyright Act which provides that collecting societies must be registered as companies limited by guarantee and under the Companies and Allied Matters Act of 2004. A company limited by guarantee is a not-for-profit company.

[16] PwC report Op Cit at footnote 11.

b. Compulsory collective management (e.g., France)—under this system rights owners are legally obliged to negotiate secondary rights through a CMO with no opt out.
3. Licensing under a legal licence. This also takes two forms:
a. Non-voluntary system with a legal licence (e.g., Switzerland). Here a licence to copy is provided by law so that no agreement with the rights owner is needed. There is a right to remuneration, however, and a statutory licence fee is set by law and collected by a CMO on behalf of all rights owners.
b. Private copying remuneration with a levy system (e.g. Belgium). Secondary licence fees are levied on copying equipment at the point of sale or for ongoing operation (e.g., for photocopiers) and the CMO collects and distributes the fees to the rights owner.[17]

The seven operating systems identified by Gervais and the three structural models mentioned in the PWC report, both dealing with CMO's operation, reflect how CMO's carry out their core mandates[18] which, in a general sense involve the monitoring of owners' works, negotiating terms of use with users, granting or issuance of licenses, collecting of royalties from users and distribution of same to right owners.[19] In the use of any of these models what must be borne in mind is that the transaction element always involves the right of the Copyright/Related Right Owner. It is therefore important that whatever structural model is adopted in the formation or reformation of a legal framework, the interest of rights' owners' should be specially considered and they should be allowed the privilege and opportunity of taking decisions in respect of the collective management of their rights.[20] Where a society provides for voting rights, caution should be taken in the investiture of voting rights[21] as such rights are best handled by those who have substantial interest in the society.[22]

[17] Ibid. It is noteworthy that the PWC report focused on literary and artistic works (i.e., books, journals, magazines and other periodicals, paintings, sculptures and other artistic works).

[18] See *Introduction To Collective Management Of Copyright And Related Rights* available online at http://uatm.com.ua/laws/int/Introduction%20to%20Collective%20Management%20of%20Copyright%20and%20Related%20Rights.pdf *Date of use*: 24 March 2012 where the core mandates of a collective management organization were highlighted as follows:- "In the framework of a collective management system, owners of rights authorize collective management organizations to administer their rights, that is, to **monitor the use** of the works concerned, **negotiate with prospective users**, **give them licenses** against appropriate fees and, under appropriate conditions, **collect such fees** and **distribute them** among the owners of rights".

[19] See for example Section 39 (8) of the Nigerian Copyright Act which provides that "collecting society means an association of copyright owners which has as its principal objectives the negotiating and granting of licenses, collecting and distributing of royalties in respect of copyright works; group of persons includes a body corporate".

[20] Uchtenhagen *The Setting up of New Copyright Societies* 17.

[21] Ibid. Ulrich suggested that only those authors and publishers with accounts exceeding a certain minimum should be granted voting rights.

[22] Ibid.

3.3 Legal Framework for Copyright Collective Administration in Nigeria

3.3.1 The 1970 Act

The first indigenous Copyright Act in Nigeria was passed in 1970.[23] The Act contained very little information on collective administration. However, the little information it contained forms the bedrock of Nigeria's legal framework for collective administration.

Section 13 of the 1970 Copyright Act had five subsections and was designated by short title as the section on "appointment and powers of competent authority". These subsections provided the following important information:

1. Appointment of three persons by the Commissioner[24] to constitute the competent authority.[25]
2. Checks and balances on a licensing body's[26] powers to grant licences[27]
3. Integrity, fairness and transparency of members of the competent authority[28]
4. Provisions for appeal to the Commissioner by any aggrieved persons[29]

[23] This Act was originally promulgated as Copyright Decree (No 61) of 1970 and later re-designated as the Copyright Act by the operation of the Adaptation of Laws (Re-designation of Decrees) Order No.13 of 1980. It repealed the 1911 Copyright Act of the United Kingdom which had been extended to Nigeria in 1912.

[24] The interpretation section of the Act (Nigeria Copyright Act 1970) defined Commissioner as the Commissioner for Trade.

[25] Section 13(1) of the Nigerian Copyright Act 1970.

[26] Section 13(2) provided an interpretation for licensing body. "In this subsession "licensing body" means a society, firm or other Organization which has its main object, or one of its main objects, the negotiation or granting of licences in respect of copyright works, and includes an individual carrying on the same activity.

[27] See Section 13(2) of the Nigerian Copyright Act 1970 which provided that where a licensing body unreasonably refuses to grant licences or is imposing unreasonable terms for the grant of licences, the competent authority may direct in relation to a work covered under the licensing bodies purview that a licence shall be deemed to have been granted by the licensing body upon payment of the prescribed fees.

[28] Section 13(3) of the Nigerian Copyright Act 1970.

[29] The section provides that the outcome of such appeal shall be final.

5. Powers to make regulation in respect of the competent authority[30]

The above provisions formed the first legal framework for Copyright Collective administration in Nigeria. This framework allowed for a voluntary licensing system[31] and also incorporated a non-voluntary or compulsory licensing system[32] allowing aggrieved users access to the work on payment of the prescribed fees. This further served as checks and balances to the licensing bodies. This is in line with IFFRO's model as enunciated in the PWC report.[33] Interestingly, the provisions of these sections were never activated[34] but their existence most likely served as deterrence to any possible abuse of power by the licensing bodies.[35] Furthermore their existence serves as *the basis* for Nigeria's first legal framework for Copyright Collective Administration.

3.3.2 The 1988 Act

The Nigerian Copyright Act 1988 was a product of industry agitations and lobby.[36] Foremost amongst the lobbyist were active players in the collective administration sector[37] who took steps to ensure that issues of collective administration were adequately captured in the draft copyright law.[38] On the 19th of December, 1988

---

30 Section 15(5) placed the powers to make regulations on the Commissioner. It listed five issues that could be covered by the regulation as follows: The Commissioner may make regulations-

1. prescribing how matters may be referred to the competent authority,
2. prescribing the procedure, records to be kept and member of the competent authority who shall preside at its sittings,
3. prescribing the manner in which the competent authority shall be convened and the place where it shall hold its sittings,
4. prescribing a scale of costs and fees, and
5. providing generally for the better carrying out of the functions assigned to the competent authority by this Decree.

31 See Section 13(2) of the Nigerian Copyright Act 1970 where the responsibility of licensing bodies was indicated as being to negotiate and grant licences. The Act does not place any conditions or restrictions to the exercise of that power.

32 Ibid. The subsection provided that where the licensing body unreasonably refused to grant a licence, the competent authority could direct that the licence sought be deemed to have been granted.

33 Op cit footnote 11.

34 Asein *Nigerian Copyright Law* 219.

35 Ibid.

36 Okoroji *Copyright, Neighbouring Rights & the New Millionaires* 167.

37 Ibid.

38 Ibid at 195 where it was said that "one of the important contents of the Draft Copyright Law submitted to the government jointly by the Nigerian Law Reform Commission and the Drafting Committee of the National Seminar on the Nigerian Copyright Law, was a provision in Section 35 for the regulation of collective administration of copyright in Nigeria".

when Decree 47 of 1988 was promulgated, "the provision for the regulation of collecting societies had been deleted".[39] The Nigerian Copyright Act 1988 therefore did not provide a legal framework for the administration of Copyright and related rights on a collective basis.

3.3.3 The 1992 Amendment to the Act

The legal framework bringing Collective Administration of Copyright and related rights under a regulatory regime can be traced back to the amendment effected on the Nigerian Copyright Act in 1992.[40] This Amendment introduced provisions for the regulation of collective administration of copyright and related rights in Nigeria. It has, in this regard been said that the provisions are basically the same with those proposed for the Nigerian Copyright Act 1988.[41]

Section 32B of the Act,[42] now Section 39 has nine subsections and covers several themes. For the purpose of this work, I have identified the following central themes as being of significance: nomenclature[43]; formation[44]; conditions for approval[45]; for-profit or not-for-profit[46]; principal activities of a collecting society[47]; single or multiple societies[48]; Illegality/criminalization of operations without requisite approval[49]; powers of the Commission to make regulations specifying

[39] See Ibid at 196 where Okoroji who was a member of the Draft Copyright Law Committee expressed surprise at the deletion of the provision purportedly drafted to regulate copyright collective administration and further noted at page 195 that MCSN's "obvious objective was to abort any attempt to regulate collective administration of copyright".

[40] Copyright Amendment Decree No.98 of 1992. See also Okoroji *Copyright, Neighbouring Rights & the New Millionaires* 167.

[41] See Okoroji *Copyright, Neighbouring Rights & the New Millionaires* 199 where he said; "Except for minor changes, the new Section 32B was in fact the same section 35 deleted from the original draft of the law".

[42] The 1998 Act as Amended in 1992 and subsequently 1999 is now known as the Nigerian Copyright Act, Chapter C28, Laws of the federation of Nigeria 2004. The 2004 laws were re-arranged, thus Section 32B of the old Act is now the current Section 39 of the Nigerian Copyright Act 2004.

[43] Section 39 is titled Collecting Society.

[44] Section 39(1) provides for formation of a collecting society and application for approval.

[45] Section 39(2)a–d provides the conditions for approving a collecting society.

[46] Section 39(2)a addresses the for-profit or not-for-profit nature of a collecting society in Nigeria.

[47] Section 39(2) and (8) are similar provisions highlighting the general duties/principal objectives of a collecting society.

[48] Section 39 (1 and 3) addresses the issue of single or multiple collecting societies in Nigeria.

[49] Section 39(4), (5) and (6) the combined reading of these subsections criminalizes the act of performing the activities of a collecting society without the approval of the Commission.

conditions to give effect to the Act.[50] The above enumerated themes constitute the operational basis for copyright collective administration in Nigeria. Other jurisdictions may apply the same or similar themes as several aspects of collective management of rights are influenced by international and national legislative and regulatory frameworks.[51] This work will attempt to analyze the legal framework for collective administration in Nigeria in light of the identified central themes.

As noted above, the enumerated central themes are based on Section 39 of the Nigerian Copyright Act. It would therefore be pertinent at this point to reproduce *holus-bolus* the provisions of the said section:

Section 39.[52] Collecting Society

1. A Collecting Society (in this section referred to as "a society") may be formed in respect of anyone or more rights of copyrights owners for the benefit of such owners, and the society may apply to the Commission for approval to operate as a collecting society for the purpose of this Act.
2. The Commission may approve a society if it is satisfied that-
   (a) it is incorporated as a company limited by guarantee;
   (b) its objects are to carry out the general duty of negotiating and granting copyright licenses and collecting royalties on behalf of copyright owners and distributing same to them;
   (c) it represents a substantial number of owners of copyright in any category of works protected by this Act; in this paragraph of this subsection, "owners of copyright" includes owners of performers' rights;
   (d) it complies with the terms and conditions prescribed by regulations made by the Commission under this section.
3. The Commission shall not approve another society in respect of any class of copyright owners, if it is satisfied that an existing approved society adequately protects the interest of that class of copyright owners.
4. It shall be unlawful for any group of persons to purport to perform the duties of a society without the approval of the Commission as required under this section of this Act.
5. Any person who contravenes the provisions of subsection (4) of this section, is guilty of an offence and liable on conviction to a fine of N1,000 on the first conviction and for any other subsequent conviction to a fine of N2,000 or to imprisonment for a term not exceeding six months or to both such fine and imprisonment.

---

[50] Section 39(7).

[51] See Gervais, *Collective Management* 26 where he identified six aspects of collective administration of rights as it relates to legal and regulatory frameworks. The six identified aspects are: (1) The legal Status of CMO's; (2) The mode of rights acquisition; (3) Legislative support, if any; (4) State Control of CMO's (formation and/or operation; (5) Tariff and licensing practices and (6) distribution practices and accounting).

[52] Section 32B of the 1988 Act is now Section 39 of the current Act (2004).

6. Where the contravention is by a body corporate, it shall be guilty of an offence and liable on conviction to a fine of N10,000 on the first conviction and N2,000 for each day on which the offence continues.
7. The Commission shall have power to make regulations specifying the conditions necessary to give effect to the purposes of this section of this Act.
8. For the purposes of this section "collecting society" means an association of copyright owners which has as its principal objectives the negotiating and granting of licenses, collecting and distributing of royalties in respect of copyright works; "group of persons" includes a body corporate.
9. The Commission may, where it finds it expedient, assist in establishing a collecting society for any class of copyright owners."

3.3.3.1 Nomenclature

The Nigerian Copyright Act designates the title "collecting society[53]" to organizations or associations of copyright owners[54] who carry out the general duties of negotiating and granting licenses, collecting and distributing royalties in respect of copyright works.[55] The effect of the combined reading of the title "Collecting Society" in Section 39 and the wording of Section 39(1) regarding the circumstances under which a collecting society may be formed, and that of Section 39 (8) providing the meaning of collecting society is to make it clear that the drafters of the Act intended that a society or an association of copyright owners having its core objectives as negotiating and granting of licenses, as well as collecting and distribution of royalties in respect of copyright owners, *should be designated under the Nigerian Copyright Act as a collecting society*. The challenges arising from the afore-mentioned nomenclature will be elaborated upon in Chap. 4.

3.3.3.2 Formation

The first subsection of Section 39 deals with the formation of a collecting society and specifically provides that a society

1. may be formed in respect of one or more rights of copyright owners;
2. should be for the benefit of such copyright owners; and
3. may apply to the Commission for approval to operate as a collecting society for the purpose of the Act.

[53] This terminology is one and the same with Collective Management Organization as the Copyright (Collective Management Organization) Regulation 2007 uses that nomenclature.

[54] The definition of a collecting society provided at Section 39(8) provides that it means an "association of copyright owners".

[55] See Section 39, 39(1) and Section 39(8).

3.3.3.3 Conditions for Approval

Section 39(2) enumerates four specific requirements a society is expected to comply with before the Commission may grant it approval to operate as a collecting society. These requirements are as follows:

1. The society is to be registered as a company limited by guarantee.
2. The object of the company should be negotiating and granting copyright licenses and collecting royalties on behalf of copyright owners and distributing same to them.
3. It should represent a substantial number of copyright owners.[56]
4. It should comply with the terms and conditions prescribed in the regulations made by the Commission in respect of copyright collective administration.

3.3.3.4 For-Profit or Not-For-Profit

Section 39(2)a provides that a society desirous of being approved as a collecting society is to be incorporated as a company limited by guarantee. A company limited by guarantee[57] is a not-for-profit entity.[58] This provision places collective administration in Nigeria under the not-for-profit model. It should be noted that different legal frameworks provide for different models in respect of whether collective administration is modeled after a for-profit or not-for-profit structure.[59] For example the Canadian collective administration system does not impose a particular legal form; consequently some collecting societies are for-profit entities but are run by not-for-profit organizations.[60] It appears that most collecting

[56] The amendment to the Act in 1999 specified "50" as the minimum number of persons a collecting society is expected to represent to entitle such a society to initiate or commence infringement actions. See Section 17 of the Nigerian Copyright Act 2004. This section was Section 15A under the old Act. At Reg 1(2)e of the CMO Regulation, a membership list of not less than 100 right owners is required from any company applying for licence to operate as a CMO.

[57] See Section 26(1) of the Companies and Allied Matters Act 1990 (hereinafter referred to as CAMA) which provides that a company limited by guarantee is one formed for the purposes of promoting commerce, art, science, religion, sports, culture, education, research, charity or other similar objects and the income and property are to be applied solely toward the promotion of its objects and no portion thereof is to be paid or transferred directly or indirectly to the members of the company except as permitted by this decree.

[58] See Section 26(4) CAMA which states that "a company limited by guarantee shall not be incorporated with the object of carrying on business for the purposes of making profits for distribution to members". Interestingly, one of the principal objectives of a collecting society is the distribution of royalties to copyright owners. A line of difference can be drawn between the distribution of profit and royalty, hence collecting societies are registered as companies limited by guarantee under CAMA.

[59] See Gervais *Collective Management* 26.

[60] Ibid.

societies are not-for-profit entities but the actual position is determined by the legal framework of each country.

3.3.3.5 Principal Activities of a Collecting Society

The activities of collecting societies revolve around the owner, their work and the users. The general principles by which collecting societies operate are underpinned by an authorization given to societies by owners of copyright, in terms of which the society is authorized to negotiate with prospective users, give them licenses against appropriate fees and under appropriate conditions, collect such fees and distribute them among the owners of rights.[61] The Nigerian Copyright Act 1988 contains similar provisions at Section 39(2)b and (8). Both provisions identify the principal activities a collecting society is expected to carry out. Four keywords are strategic with regard to the referred activities. The four keywords are *negotiating* (licenses), *granting* (licenses), *collecting* (royalties), and *distributing* (royalties). It is however noteworthy that not all collecting societies perform these activities in respect of all works, as the nature of some works (such as dramatic works) do not require that collecting societies negotiate and grant licence on their behalf. They however often use the collecting society's platform for collection and distribution of royalties.[62]

3.3.3.6 Single or Multiple Societies

The Nigerian Copyright Act provides at Section 39(1) that the formation of a collecting society may be "in respect of any one or more rights of copyright owners". It further provides at Section 39(3) that "the Commission shall not approve another Society in respect of any class of copyright owners if it is satisfied that an existing approved society adequately protects the interest of that class of copyright owners." The wording of the Nigerian Copyright Act in this regard is quite intriguing. On the one hand, it refers to a society being formed *in respect of one or more rights* S.39 (1); on the other, it then notes that the Commission would not approve another society "*in respect of any class of copyright owners*" S.39 (3). The first subsection makes it clear that a collecting society may administer one or more rights, therefore a single society may administer multiple rights. The question to ask therefore is, "Can multiple societies administer the same rights or administer rights in respect of the same class of copyright owners?". In attempting to capture this issue within a legal framework, the drafters of the Act made it clear

[61] See *Introduction To Collective Management Of Copyright And Related Rights* available online at http://uatm.com.ua/laws/int/Introduction%20to%20Collective%20Management%20of%20Copyright%20and%20Related%20Rights.pdf *Date of use: 26 March 2012*".

[62] Ibid at paragraph 21 page 5.

that approval shall not be given to another society *in respect of any class of copyright owners* if the existing approved society *adequately protects the interest of that class of copyright owners*. The wording however leaves the question open as to whether there is a difference between administration of copyright based on rights and that based on class of copyright owners. That question can be left for another time. What is important to note here is that the Commission would not approve another society if it satisfied with the existing one. It can thus be implied that where the Commission is not satisfied with the existing one, a second may be approved. If that is the case, it implies therefore that multiple societies may be approved in respect of the same class of copyright owners. In the author's assessment of the legal framework relating to single and multiple societies in the Act, it appears that the Act tends to favor a single society model, while leaving room for multiple societies under stringent and very narrow conditions.

3.3.3.7 Illegality/Criminalization of Operations Without Requisite Approval

Obtaining approval to operate as a collecting society is taken very seriously under the Nigerian Copyright Act.[63] Failure to obtain approval is an unlawful act and punishable with a fine of N1,000 on the first conviction and N2,000 on subsequent ones, or to a term of imprisonment not exceeding 6 months or to both the fine and imprisonment.[64] Where it is a body corporate found guilty of the offence, it is liable on conviction to a fine of N10,000 on the first conviction and to N2,000 for each day the offence continues.[65]

3.3.3.8 Powers to Make Regulation

The Nigerian Copyright Act gives the Nigerian Copyright Commission discretionary powers to make regulations which would specify certain conditions required for effective copyright collective administration of rights in Nigeria.[66] In furtherance of this power, the Nigerian Copyright Commission issued a collecting society regulation which will be reviewed hereunder.

---

[63] Section 39(4) Nigerian Copyright Act.

[64] Section 39(5) Nigerian Copyright Act.

[65] Section 39(6) Nigerian Copyright Act.

[66] See Section 39(7) Nigerian Copyright Act.

3.3.4 The Copyright (Collecting Societies) Regulations, 1993

The provision for activating an additional or supplementary mechanism for the effective implementation of copyright collective administration in Nigeria is as contained in Section 39 of the Nigerian Copyright Act.[67] Taking cognizance of the need of the industry,[68] the Nigerian Copyright Commission on the 16th of August, 1993 issued the Copyright (Collecting Societies) Regulation 1993. This instrument has now been revoked by virtue of the coming into force of a new collecting society regulation.[69] Notwithstanding the new regulation, an analysis of the old is pertinent, as the new regulation builds on the old one and the experiences in the industry have been with regard to the old.

The Copyright (Collecting Societies) Regulation 1993 had seventeen regulations, all of which were targeted at giving effect to the provisions of the parent enactment, that is, Section 39 of the Nigerian Copyright Act. The Regulations provided further details regarding the processes for approval to operate as a society[70] and for the granting of licences.[71] Further to this it provided for the internal mechanisms of a collecting society,[72] settlement of Tariff disputes,[73] Renewals,[74] and withdrawals of Approval.[75]

3.3.4.1 Approval and Grant of Licence

The Regulations elaborated on the application process and provided detailed information on how an interested applicant was to make an application. In addition to the type of company to be registered and the object of its activities, the Regulations went further to lay out other requirements to be fulfilled as follows:

1. Applications are to be in the prescribed form[76]
2. The prescribed fees must be paid[77]

---

[67] Ibid.

[68] Shyllon *Intellectual Property Law in Nigeria* 130.

[69] The Copyright (Collective Management Organization) Regulations 2007 at Regulation 21 revoked the copyright (Collecting Societies) Regulation 1993.

[70] Regulation 4, Copyright (Collecting Societies) Regulation, 1993.

[71] Regulation 6, Copyright (Collecting Societies) Regulation, 1993.

[72] Regulations 11, 12, and 13, Copyright (Collecting Societies) Regulation, 1993.

[73] Regulation 15, Copyright (Collecting Societies) Regulation, 1993.

[74] Regulation 16, Copyright (Collecting Societies) Regulation, 1993.

[75] Regulation 17, Copyright (Collecting Societies) Regulation, 1993.

[76] Regulation 4 (1) Copyright (Collecting Societies) Regulation, 1993.

[77] Ibid.

3. An application for approval must be signed by 2 principals officers of the company or its authorized agent[78]
4. Interested applicants must furnish the following documents[79]
a. Certificate of registration issued under CAMA[80]
b. The memorandum of association of the Company[81]
c. The articles of association of the Company[82]
d. Such other documents as may be required[83]
5. Subscribers to the memorandum shall not be less than 10 persons[84]
6. The organs of the company shall comprise at least a governing board and a management board[85]
7. The Chief Executive Officer shall not be a member of the society[86]
8. A member of the council[87] shall be included on the Management board of the company[88]
9. The Chairman must be a member of the society[89]
10. Must show proof of evidence of adequate and competent staff[90]

3.3.4.2 Single or Multiple Societies

The Regulation also addresses the issue of multiple societies in respect of any class of copyright owners and it provides that under such a situation, after due investigation, only one of the societies which "in its opinion, will more adequately protect

[78] See Regulation 4 (2), Copyright (Collecting Societies) Regulation, 1993 which provides that the authorized agent must be a legal practitioner.

[79] Regulation 4 (3), Copyright (Collecting Societies) Regulation, 1993.

[80] Regulation 4 (3)a Copyright (Collecting Societies) Regulation, 1993. The certificate of incorporation of a company is prima facie evidence that the company has been registered. See Section 36(6) CAMA. Certificates of registration are issued by the Corporate Affairs Commission, the agency established by CAMA.

[81] Regulation 4 (3)b, Copyright (Collecting Societies) Regulation, 1993. The memorandum of association is expected among other things to contain the object of business of a company, in the case of a collecting society, its proposed principal aims and objectives. See Section 27(1)c.

[82] Regulation 4 (3)c, Copyright (Collecting Societies) Regulation, 1993. The registration of the memorandum and articles of association has the effect of a contract under seal. See Section 41(1) CAMA.

[83] Regulation 4 (3)d, Copyright (Collecting Societies) Regulation, 1993.

[84] Regulation 6(1)a, Copyright (Collecting Societies) Regulation, 1993.

[85] Regulation 6 (1)b, Copyright (Collecting Societies) Regulation, 1993.

[86] Regulation 6 (1)c, Copyright (Collecting Societies) Regulation, 1993.

[87] In 1995, the Nigerian Copyright Council was changed to Nigerian Copyright Commission.

[88] Regulation 6 (1)d, Copyright (Collecting Societies) Regulation, 1993.

[89] Regulation 6 (1)e, Copyright (Collecting Societies) Regulation, 1993.

[90] Regulation 6 (1)f, Copyright (Collecting Societies) Regulation, 1993.

the interests of the class of right owners" shall be approved.[91] The implication of the provision of this regulation read in conjunction with that of the main Act[92] is that at the stage of application, the Commission will not approve two collecting societies simultaneously. However, as the Act implies, where the Commission is not satisfied with the performance of the existing society, it may approve another.[93]

3.3.4.3 Approval, Renewal, and Withdrawal

Upon satisfactory compliance with the requirement of the Commission, the application is approved and a certificate of approval is issued to the applicant.[94] Approval is valid for a period of 3 years[95] in the first instance and renewed for another period of three years on such terms as may be specified.[96] The Council may however withdraw the certificate of approval granted a collecting society where such society has ceased to function as a collecting society. The withdrawal is effected by a notice of withdrawal.[97]

3.3.4.4 Internal Mechanism

Reports of minutes of the General Assembly and management board is expected to be recorded in a special register and a certified true copy of same sent to the Council within three months of such recordal.[98] Furthermore the society is expected to keep proper accounts[99] of payments, credits, and liabilities but is permitted to withhold 30 % of the total royalties and fees collected during the year as administrative fees.[100]

---

91 Regulation 7 (2), Copyright (Collecting Societies) Regulation, 1993.

92 Section 39(3) Nigerian Copyright Act states "The commission shall not approve another society in respect of any class of copyright owners, it is satisfied that an existing approved society adequately protects the interest of that class of copyright owners.

93 In this regard it may be useful to consider what was said earlier at Para 3.3.3.6 above.

94 Regulation 9, Copyright (Collecting Societies) Regulation, 1993.

95 Regulation 10, Copyright (Collecting Societies) Regulation, 1993.

96 Regulation 16, Copyright (Collecting Societies) Regulation, 1993.

97 Regulation 17, Copyright (Collecting Societies) Regulation, 1993.

98 Regulation 11, Copyright (Collecting Societies) Regulation, 1993.

99 Regulation 12 (1), Copyright (Collecting Societies) Regulation, 1993.

100 Regulation 12 (2), Copyright (Collecting Societies) Regulation, 1993.

3.3.4.5 Settlement of Tariffs

The Regulations provide a mechanism for the settlement of tariff disputes between users and the collecting society.[101] In this regard it provides for a Tariffs Arbitration Panel[102] to resolve disputes. The Regulations provide for the number of the Panel[103] and how it shall be constituted[104] and empowers the Council to make Regulations providing for its mode of operation.[105] The Regulations further provides that the decision of the Panel is final and binding upon the parties, subject to the right of appeal to the Federal High Court on points of law.[106]

3.3.5 1999 Amendment to the Act

In 1999, the Copyright Act was further amended[107] to limit the right of action on infringement of copyright. The amendment was to the effect that no collecting society shall commence or maintain an action for the infringement of copyright unless such action was approved by the Commission and unless such collecting society represents more than 50 owners of copyright.[108] This amendment introduced the cardinal issue of "representation of not less than 50 owners of copyright" for purposes of commencing or maintaining an action for infringement of Copyright and reinforced the provisions of the amendment made in 1992 in respect of prior approval to operate as a collecting society. In the case of "Musical Copyright Society Nigeria Ltd v Details Nigeria Limited",[109] an *ex-parte* order had been obtained by the plaintiff against the defendants to which the defendant raised a *locus standi* objection. The defendant argued that since the plaintiff had claimed to represent more than two million artistes, and was essentially carrying out the activities of negotiating and granting of licenses, collection and distribution of royalties on copyright works, the plaintiff was functioning as a collecting society and required the approval of the Nigerian Copyright Commission to operate as a collecting society in order to be entitled to institute copyright infringement proceedings. The plaintiff on the other hand denied commencing the action as a collecting society but rather as an owner, assignee, and exclusive licensee as contemplated under Section 15 of the Act.[110] The court in

---

[101] Regulation 15 (1), Copyright (Collecting Societies) Regulation, 1993.

[102] Ibid.

[103] Regulation 15 (2), Copyright (Collecting Societies) Regulation, 1993.

[104] Ibid.

[105] Regulation 15 (4), Copyright (Collecting Societies) Regulation, 1993.

[106] Regulation 15 (5), Copyright (Collecting Societies) Regulation, 1993.

[107] Copyright Amendment Decree No.42 1999.

[108] Section 15A. The provision in the current Act is now Section 17.

[109] (1996) F.H.C.L.R 473.

[110] This provision is now Section 16 under the current law.

arriving at its decision, having considered the evidence tendered, for instance the deed of assignments executed in favor of MCSN which enunciated the aims, objectives and functions of the company, ruled as follows:

> I have come to the inexorable conclusion ...that the plaintiff is a collecting society. Not having been registered pursuant to Section 32B(4) of the Copyright Act, it cannot be permitted to operate as such a body. To do so would be tantamount to subverting not only the letter but also the spirit of the copyright laws of this country.[111]

3.3.6 Copyright (Collective Management Organization) Regulation 2007

3.3.6.1 Introduction

The withdrawal of the licence granted to MCSN triggered several protests from MCSN and other stakeholders leading to a crisis in the affected industry.[112] In a bid to resolving these crises, several meetings were held, none of which unfortunately produced the desired result. The several failed attempts at resolving the crisis in collective administration in the Music Industry kept haunting the Commission and indeed the whole Copyright Industry.[113] When the last of these attempts, like the others, failed, a meeting was held aimed at putting a final end to these disputes.[114] The meeting, which was specially directed by the Honorable Attorney General of the Federation and Minister for Justice,[115] resolved that the Commission take all necessary steps to resolve the crisis of collective management in the Music industry.[116] In view of this, a review of the legal framework for collective administration in Nigeria was embarked upon by the Commission.[117]

---

[111] On this matter see also the similar judgment of Jinadu J in MCSN v Nigeria Hotels Suit No FHC/L/43/89.

[112] Okoroji *Copyright Neighbouring Rights and The New Millionaires* 180.

[113] See Adewopo, *Nigerian Copyright System: Principles and Perspectives* 106 where he noted that "the above development culminated in a zero collective administration state in the music industry, which situation has foisted a situation of complete helplessness on the innocent right owners and artistes in the music industry." See also Okoroji *Copyright Neighbouring Rights and The New Millionaires* 182.

[114] The meeting was held at the Topview Hotel, Abuja. The resolution was made on the last day of the meeting, on May 22, 2007.

[115] Chief Bayo Ojo was the Honorable Attorney General of the Federation and Minister for Justice at the time.

[116] See Generally Adewopo, *Nigerian Copyright System: Principles and Perspectives* 106 and Okoroji *Copyright Neighbouring Rights and The New Millionaires* 182.

[117] Adewopo, *Nigerian Copyright System: Principles and Perspectives* 106 and (Okoroji Op Cit at 241).

After a very rigorous exercise[118] and upon obtaining the consent of the Supervising Minister, the Copyright (Collective Management Organization) Regulation was issued[119] and published in the Federal Republic of Nigeria official gazette,[120] pursuant to Section 39(7) of the Nigerian Copyright Act. The Regulation comprises four parts, twenty-three provisions and a schedule. The first part provides for the grant of licences (application, revocation and renewal of licences); Membership and Management of the organization is provided for in the second part, while Licensing, Distribution of royalties and Miscellaneous Provisions are captured in the third and fourth parts. The 2007 Regulation revoked the Copyright (Collecting Societies) Regulation 1993 and changed the nomenclature of societies carrying on the business of copyright collective management from collecting societies to CMOs.[121] Section 39 of the Nigerian Copyright Act in conjunction with the 2007 regulation provides the legal and regulatory framework for the administration of collective management organizations in Nigeria.

3.3.6.2 Grant of Licence

Part 1 of the CMO regulation provides for the grant of licences. It provides for the requirements and conditions for application, revocation and renewal of licences.

Application

An interested applicant may apply[122] in the prescribed form[123] upon payment of the prescribed fees.[124] In addition to the above requirements of the Regulation[125] every company applying for licence to operate as a CMO shall furnish the Commission with the following documents:

1. "a Certificate of registration in respect of the company issued under the Companies and Allied Matters Act;
2. the Memorandum of Association of the Company;
3. the Articles of Association of the Company

---

[118] Ibid.

[119] On the 28th of September, 2007.

[120] as No.98 of volume 94, on the 3rd of October, 2007.

[121] See Regulation 22 where Collective Management Organization was interpreted to mean Collecting Society.

[122] Regulation 1 Copyright (Collective Management Organizations) Regulations 2007 (hereinafter referred to as CMO Reg).

[123] The prescribed form is attached to the regulation as a schedule and tagged FORM NCC/CSR 1.

[124] See Regulation 18 CMO Reg.

[125] See Regulation 1 CMO Reg.

4. a Statement indicating the class of right or category of right owners in which the society owns rights, or intends to represent or act for;
5. membership list of not less than 100 right owners representing the class(es) of right to which the company is seeking a licence to operate as a CMO, which list shall indicate the signed consent of such persons to belong to the Organization, or where the Organization has been in existence, that they are members of the society;
6. Undertakings by at least five Directors including the Chairman of the Company that the Company shall comply with provisions of the Copyright Act and these Regulations in respect of the operations of the Organization;
7. membership agreement used by the Organization;
8. evidence of payment of the prescribed fee(s); and
9. such other documents as may be required by the Commission."

The new regulation provides for further requirements to be met prior to the acceptance of an application. The old regulation had provided for six requirements to be met prior to the grant of an approval,[126] but the new regulation added the following requirements:

1. All requirements as stipulated by the Act and the CMO regulation have been met[127];
2. Organs of the company to comprise at least a General Assembly and a Governing Board[128];
3. The Chief Executive Officer shall not be a member of the company, should be knowledgeable in copyright matters and approved by the Commission as competent to run the affairs of a CMO.[129]
4. The Management to be approved as competent to run the affairs of a CMO[130];
5. The memorandum of association to provide the main function of the Organization to be the administration of collective management of copyright[131];
6. The articles of association provides for attendance of the Commission's representative at the Governing Board and other general meetings as an observer[132]

---

[126] See Regulation 6 (1)a–f Copyright (Collecting Societies Regulation) 1993 which provided that the subscribers to the memorandum of association shall not be less than 10 persons with proven interests in the areas which the company desires to operate as a collecting society. The organs of the company to comprise a General Assembly and a management Board; the Chief Executive Officer of the company must not be a member of the society; the Management Board of the company shall include one member of the Commission; the Chairman of the Management Board must be a member of the society; evidence of adequate and competent staff.

[127] Regulation 1 (3)a CMO Reg.

[128] Regulation 1(3)b CMO Reg.

[129] Regulation 1 (3)c CMO Reg.

[130] Regulation 1 (3)d CMO Reg.

[131] Regulation 1 (3)e CMO Reg.

[132] Regulation 1(3)f CMO Reg.

7. The Chairman of the Governing Board must be a member of the Organization[133]
8. The Governing Board and Management of the CMO consist of citizens of Nigeria and ordinarily resident in Nigeria.[134]

The CMO regulation introduced the requirement of obtaining approval as to the competence of the Chief Executive Officer and the Management of the Organization. It further requires that both the Governing Board and the Management of the Organization shall consist of persons who are Nigerian citizens and ordinarily resident in Nigeria.

The new Regulation by the introduction of the seven under-listed additional requirements raises the regulatory bar and seeks to ensure that organizations seeking to operate as collective management organizations meet the set standards.

1. A statement indicating the class of right or category of right owners in which the society owns rights, or intends to represent or act for[135];
2. Membership list of not less than 100 right owners[136];
3. Undertaking by at least five Directors including the chairman of the company[137];
4. Membership agreement[138];
5. Obtain approval as to the competence of the CEO[139];
6. Obtain approval as to the competence of the Management of the Organization[140];
7. The Governing Board and Management of the Organization to be comprised of persons who are citizens of Nigeria and ordinarily resident in Nigeria.

Where an applicant satisfies the above requirements and other requirements stipulated in the Act and the Regulation, the Commission may accept its application and upon approval issue it with a certificate as evidence of its license to operate as a collective management organization.[141] If the Commission is not satisfied, it may refuse to grant a license.[142] In the event of a refusal and at the request of the applicant, the Commission shall provide in writing the grounds for its decision.[143]

---

133 Regulation 1 (3)g CMO Reg.

134 Regulation 1 (3)h CMO Reg.

135 See Regulation 2 (d) CMO Reg.

136 See Regulation 2 (e) CMO Reg.

137 See Regulation 2 (f) CMO Reg.

138 See Regulation 2 (g) CMO Reg.

139 See Regulation 1 (3)c CMO Reg.

140 See Regulation 1 (3)d CMO Reg.

141 See Regulation 1 (5) CMO Reg.

142 See Regulation 1 (6) CMO Reg.

143 See Regulation 1 (8) CMO Reg.

Renewal

All licences to operate as a collective management organization are valid for 3 years and renewable every 2 years.[144] The regulation encourages that applications for renewal be made anytime within six months before the expiration of its license.[145] Renewal of a license is subject to the discretion of the Commission.[146]

Revocation

The Commission, on its own motion or upon an application by an interested person, may revoke a license if the organization contravenes or fails to comply with any provision of the Act, the Regulations, a direction or order made or given to it under the Regulations, or the organization no longer represents the interests of the copyright owners for which license was granted to it.[147]

3.3.6.3 Membership and Management of Collective Management Organizations

The CMO Regulation provides that each member of the organization is entitled to one vote,[148] and makes it mandatory for the organizations to open membership to all Copyright owners of the category of works or class(es) of rights[149] to which the collective management organization administers rights and shall not impose conditions requiring a member to constitute the organization as such member's sole collecting agent.[150] Any organization found in breach of the above provisions is liable to a fine of N50,000.[151]

The regulation makes it mandatory that within 30 days of alteration to the memorandum and articles of association or any internal rules; adoption of tariffs and any alteration thereof; reciprocal representation agreements with foreign collecting societies; any alteration to the standard membership agreement; any judicial decisions or official proceedings, the organizations shall furnish the Commission with the relevant information.[152]

---

144 See Regulation 1 (9) CMO Reg.

145 See Regulation 3 (1) CMO Reg.

146 See Regulation 3 (2&3) CMO Reg which provides that "The Commission may, refuse to approve an application for renewal of a licence if, it is of the opinion that the CMO no longer meets the requirement for grant of licence".

147 See Regulation 2 CMO Reg.

148 See Regulation 5 (1) CMO Reg.

149 See Regulation 4 (1) CMO Reg.

150 See Regulation 4 (2) CMO Reg.

151 See Regulation 4(5) CMO Reg.

152 See Regulation 7 (1) CMO Reg.

Proper account reports and books consistent with ordinary accounting commercial standards shall be kept.[153] A general report of activities and an annual audited financial report should be prepared and submitted to the Commission not later than the first day of July in each year.[154] In the same vein, every meeting of the general assembly and the governing board of the society is to be entered in a special register and a certified copy of same needs to be submitted to the Commission when required.[155]

The Regulation further provides for the establishment of a Holding account to hold any share of the distributable amount which cannot be allocated or distributed.[156] At the expiration of the holding period,[157] the undistributed amount falls into the general revenue.[158]

The regulation also provides for administrative costs and notes that CMO's may withhold not more than 30 % of the total royalties and fees collected to cover administrative costs.[159]

3.3.6.4 Licensing and Distribution of Royalties

The Regulation mandates the collective management organizations to make available to users on non-discriminatory terms, their complete repertoire of works[160] with respect to which it is representing the right owners and to draw up tariffs[161] for usage of copyright works administered by them.[162] In setting tariffs, an Organization may take into consideration the following:

1. "the monetary advantage obtained from the exploitation;
2. the value of the copyright material;
3. the purpose for which, and context in which, the copyright material is used;
4. the manner or kind of use of the copyright material;
5. the proportion of the utilization of a work in the context of exploitation;
6. any relevant decision of the Court or the Dispute Resolution Panel; and
7. any other relevant matter"[163]

---

153 See Regulation 9 (1) CMO Reg.

154 See Regulation 7 (2) CMO Reg.

155 See Regulation 8 CMO Reg.

156 See Regulation 11 CMO Reg.

157 See Regulation 12 (1) CMO Reg which provides a maximum period of 7 years as the holding period.

158 See Regulation 12 (2) CMO Reg.

159 See Regulation 10 CMO Reg.

160 See Regulation 13 (1) CMO Reg.

161 See Regulation 13 (3) CMO Reg where issues to be taken into consideration are enumerated.

162 See Regulation 13 (2) CMO Reg.

163 Regulation 13 (3)a–g.

CMO's may enter into agreements with trade associations concerning the use of its repertoire by members of such trade associations.[164] Where tariff scales are accepted under such agreements, the CMO shall notify the Commission accordingly.

In the event of a dispute, the Regulation provides for a Dispute Resolution Panel to settle the dispute.[165] The panel is governed by rules as provided in the Copyright (Dispute Resolution Panel) Rules, 2007.[166]

A fair and equitable distribution plan predicated on a procedure acceptable to members and information from users must be put in place and royalties collected are expected to be distributed in a manner reflecting as nearly as possible, the actual usage of works covered by a society's repertoire.[167]

3.3.6.5 Miscellaneous Provisions

The fourth part of the regulation among other things identifies unethical practices,[168] provides for enforcement of sanctions[169] as well as a safeguard for users who are unable to make use of the license issued to them by a collective management organization by ascribable to the organization and not themselves. Under such circumstances the Regulation provides for compensation, refund or other arrangements.[170]

Compensation to Licensees

The Regulation contemplates a situation where a user is unable to utilize a licence issued to it by a CMO, by no fault of the user, but by reason of the CMO's negligence, misrepresentation or other such fault traceable to the CMO. In such a situation, the CMO is expected to provide for compensation, refund or other arrangements.

Unethical Practices

The Regulation introduced entirely new provisions in the legal framework for collective administration in Nigeria and pays attention to the conducts or practices of

---

164 Regulation 13(4).

165 See Regulation 14 CMO Reg.

166 Issued on the 2nd October 2007, Government Notice No.66 Vol 94 P B429-438.

167 See Regulation 15 CMO Reg.

168 See Regulation 17 CMO Reg.

169 See Regulation 18 CMO Reg.

170 See Regulation 16 CMO Reg.

CMO's by making unethical for instance, the granting of licences for works for which it is not authorized to administer[171]; collecting and/or distributing or purporting to collect and/or distribute royalties in respect of works for which it is not authorized to administer.[172] Other conducts or practices deemed unethical include; making false representation in respect of any matter to which it is required to provide information, knowing such representation to be false[173]; licensing discrimination to members of the same user class, either in terms of such licence or differential tariff rate[174]; inducing a user who is in the process of negotiating for a licence with another Organization or right owner, to refrain from completing the licensing process[175]; failure to make available to any other CMO information which is reasonably required by such other CMO to enable it effectively administer the rights held by it[176]; using information obtained from a CMO otherwise than as stipulated in the regulations[177] and the doing of anything or acting in a manner that has the effect of preventing any other CMO from carrying out its approved functions.[178]

3.3.6.6 Regulatory Responsibilities of the Commission

As indicated above, the 2007 CMO Regulation has apparently raised the regulatory bar on CMO's as well as the responsibilities of the Commission toward the CMOs and the public at large. A summary of the Commission's regulatory roles in this regard are as follows:-

1. Assessing and verifying additional application documents such as the statement indicating the class of right or category of right owners in which the society owns rights, or intends to represent or act for,[179] membership list

---

[171] Regulation 17 (1)a CMO Reg.

[172] Regulation 17 (1)b CMO Reg.

[173] Regulation 17 (1)c CMO Reg.

[174] See Regulation 17 (1)d CMO Reg where it was noted that "discriminating in the provision of licence to members of the same user class, either in the terms of such licence, or differential tariff rate, except such differential treatment can be reasonably justified, based on peculiar facts and circumstances applicable to the said user class".

[175] Regulation 17 (1)e CMO Reg.

[176] See Regulation 17 (1)f CMO Reg where it was noted that such information may include but is not limited to:

1. information regarding the repertoire of an author who has assigned works to both Collective Management Organization;
2. information held by a Collective Management Organization that may assist the requesting Collective Management in the computation and equitable distribution of royalties; and
3. information on the existing reciprocal representation agreement if any of a Collective Management Organization.

[177] Regulation 17 (1)g CMO Reg.

[178] Regulation 17 (1)h CMO Reg.

[179] Regulation 1 (2)d CMO Reg.

which must comprise not less than 100 right owners,[180] undertaking by at least 5 Directors inclusive of the Chairman to comply with the provisions of the Act and the CMO regulation[181] and the membership agreement.[182]

2. Approval of the Chief Executive Officer of the organization as competent to run the affairs of the organization.[183]
3. Approval of the Management of the organization as competent to run the affairs of the organization.[184]
4. Attendance at governing board and other general meetings of the organization.[185]
5. Discretion to revoke a licence.[186]
6. Acceptance of license subject to modifications.[187]
7. Renewal of licences.[188]
8. Receiving notification of certain happenings.[189]
9. Oversight on general report of the organization's activities.[190]
10. Oversight on annual audited report of the organization's activities.[191]
11. Oversight on the use of administrative fees.[192]
12. Oversight functions on licensing and tariff issues.[193]
13. Settlement of disputes.[194]
14. Administration of the Copyright (Dispute Resolution Panel) Rules, 2007.[195]
15. Enforcement of sanctions.[196]
16. Prescription of fees.[197]

---

[180] Regulation 1 (2)e CMO Reg.

[181] Regulation 1 (2)f CMO Reg.

[182] Regulation 1(2)g CMO Reg.

[183] Regulation 1 (3)c CMO Reg. It should be noted that neither the Nigerian Copyright Act nor the Regulations (Old or New) provides the yardstick for determining competence. The provisions within this particular subsection that the CEO be knowledgeable in copyright matters may provide some guidance as to competence. Following this provision, the standard for judging competence may be assessed against the level of copyright knowledge possessed by the aspiring CEOs.

[184] Regulation 1 (3)d CMO Reg. This particular regulation provides no guide as to the determination of competence. Reference may however be made to Regulation 1(3)c for guidance.

[185] Regulation 1 (3)f CMO Reg.

[186] Regulation 2 CMO Reg.

[187] Regulation 1(4) CMO Reg.

[188] Regulation 1 (9) and Regulation 3 CMO Reg.

[189] Regulation 7 (1) CMO Reg.

[190] Regulation 7 (2)a CMO Reg.

[191] Regulation 7 (2)b CMO Reg.

[192] Regulation 10 CMO Reg.

[193] Regulation 13 (5) CMO Reg.

[194] Regulation 14 CMO Reg.

[195] Regulation 14 CMO Reg and Copyright (Dispute Resolution Panel) Rules 2007.

[196] Regulation 19 CMO Reg.

[197] Regulation 18 CMO Reg.

3.3.6.7 Conclusion

The influence of the various statutes and regulations mentioned above on the legal and regulatory framework for collective administration in Nigeria has been interesting, starting from 1970 when the first indigenous Copyright Act was enacted introducing a voluntary licensing and compulsory licensing model. The intrigue that characterized the events leading to the exclusion of provisions on collective administration in 1988 created a loophole in the legal framework, which was soon corrected in 1992 with the inclusion of Section 32B. The introduction of Section 32B could be said to be the point when a proper legal framework for collective administration in Nigeria was put in place. That enactment introduced a government supervisory role over collective administration in Nigeria. The law also prescribed by implication that collecting societies shall be not-for-profit organizations and tilted the provisions of the law to favor a single society model as opposed to multiple societies. It however allows for a single society to administer multiple rights. All other amendments to the law continue to build on the framework that was set in 1992. However, as noted in the introduction to this chapter, where the people for whom laws are made do not believe in and/or accept the laws, the drafters of the law may need to go back to the drawing board. It has, at this stage, to be mentioned that the several amendments to the Act have still not yielded the desired result of an effective and harmonious collective administration system in Nigeria. One therefore wonders whether the introduction of higher regulatory measures has achieved the objective for the establishment of collecting societies and whether it has helped copyright collective administration in Nigeria.

Chapter 4
Regulatory Challenges of Collective Management in Nigeria

4.1 Background

On 22nd of July 2006 a newspaper publication[1] published an interview of the then Director General[2] of the Nigerian Copyright Commission who had just been recalled from a 3.5 months suspension. In the course of the interview, the reinstated Director General was asked as to what had really gone wrong and why he was suspended. In response, he answered:

> It was the controversy about collecting society [sic]. We approved another collecting society, the MCSN. Of course, one would expect that certain interests would be threatened. It was unfortunate in the sense that when you look at the global picture, the issue will be: Are these people not the rightful owners? Is there any superior right owner? But we should look beyond these conflicts and look at the artistes themselves. What we have seen in the last ten years is not too good for stakeholders in the music industry because we have artistes who are unable to earn money in form of royalties for the use of their works. So, we should not personalize issues. What we should focus on is how we can develop this industry; how we can create wealth and how we can ensure that we fight piracy, which is killing everybody, including the economy.[3]

The central theme of this chapter is encapsulated in part in the first sentence of the aforementioned response of the Copyright Commission Director General, in particular the phrase "the controversy about collecting society". This controversy was responsible for the suspension of the Director General in question[4] and has been said to be responsible for the death of one of the past Director Generals.[5] In fact, it has constituted a challenge to all Director Generals who have administered the affairs of the Commission.[6] This controversy dates back to when the first indigenous Nigerian

---

[1] Kolapo and Oduntan 2006-2007-22 Saturday Punch A3.
[2] Adebambo Adewopo was the Director General of the Commission at the time.
[3] Kolapo and Oduntan supra 1.
[4] Ibid.
[5] See Okoroji, *Copyright, Neighboring Rights and The New Millionaires* 176 where he implied that the death of Dr S.O. Williams was not unconnected to the controversy about collecting societies.
[6] See Okoroji, Op cit (footnote 5) 178 where it was said that "Nwauche's other tough challenge was to control the unapproved and now militant MCSN". He further noted that "at a point it was all out war between MCSN and NCC. Many believe that this may have aided Nwauche's earlier than expected departure from the NCC in June 2004".

O. Ola, *Copyright Collective Administration in Nigeria*, SpringerBriefs in Law,
DOI: 10.1007/978-3-642-35819-7_4, © The Author(s) 2013

Copyright Act was enacted in 1970.[7] At that time, no specific agency was established to oversee the administration of copyright, and neither was any provision made in respect of regulatory supervisory responsibilities in respect of collective administration in Nigeria. The Act only dealt with the appointment and powers of a "competent authority,"[8] whose role was a tangential one, dealing only with dissatisfaction regarding the grant of licenses. It has been said that this provision was actually never activated[9] which implied that there was little or no disputes that involved government's intervention. Although the government did not need to constitute the competent authority, the stakeholders in the industry had their personal grievances.[10] The challenge at the time was of the structure that was responsible for administration of copyright collective administration in Nigeria.[11] The impression of most stakeholders was that the agency run by the law firm of Alhaji Giwa existed to serve the imperialistic interest of the British, and hence local users were hesitant to pay the agency for use of works in which copyright subsists.[12] With the benefit of hindsight these "challenges" were but the tip of the iceberg in comparison with the events that ensued after the enactment of legislative provisions creating a legal and regulatory framework for the collective administration of copyright and related rights in Nigeria.

The evolution of collective administration in Nigeria was traced in Chap. 2 and the major actors on that stage were mentioned as follows: The Musical Copyright Society Nigeria Limited by Guarantee (MCSN), Performing and Mechanical Rights Society of Nigeria Ltd/Gte (PMRS) now Copyright Society of Nigeria (COSON), and Reproductions Rights Organisation of Nigeria (REPRONIG). The major challenges in collective administration of copyright and related rights have centered around one of these organizations, namely MCSN. This is not to say that the other organizations have not been embroiled in challenges as well.

4.2 Challenges from Legal and Regulatory Framework

In Chap. 3 we discussed the legal and regulatory frameworks for collective administration in Nigeria as provided for in both the principal statute[13] and the Regulation.[14] The enactments set up a legal and regulatory framework that has

[7] Decree No. 61 of 1970.

[8] Section 13 Nigerian Copyright Act 1970.

[9] Asein *Nigerian Copyright Law* 219.

[10] Okoroji Op cit (footnote 5) 192.

[11] Ibid where it was explained that a law firm, Giwa and Atilade and Co (hereinafter referred to as the agency) entered an agency agreement with PRS to represent PRS' interest in Nigeria.

[12] Ibid.

[13] Section 32B of the 1988 Nigerian Copyright Act, now section 39 of the current enactment.

[14] Formerly the Copyright (Collecting Societies Regulation) 1993 now Copyright (Collective Management Organizations) Regulation 2007 which revoked the 1993 regulations.

thrown up certain challenges relating to the implementation of the said framework. The major areas of concern have been the following:

1. Prior approval by the Commission for an organization to function as a collecting society[15] and the attendant criminal sanctions for noncompliance[16]
2. The notion of Monopoly against liberalization of the Nigerian collective administration system.

4.3 Approval Powers of the Commission

When the agency agreement between PRS of London and Giwa & co was terminated in 1986, MCSN which had been established prior to this time,[17] signed a contract of reciprocal representation with PRS,[18] thereby obtaining exclusive rights within the Nigerian territory to the repertoire of PRS.[19] Effectively, the MCSN thus carried out its activities without recourse to any statutory, supervisory, or regulatory requirements. At this time MCSN thus practiced what Gervais describes as full voluntary licensing,[20] one of the models prescribed by the International Federation of Reproductions Rights Organization.[21] By 1992, however, it had become illegal[22] and in fact a criminal offence[23] for any organization to carry on the duties of negotiating and granting of licensing as well as collecting and distributing royalties on copyright works to owners of copyright and related rights without the prior approval of the Nigerian Copyright Commission. The MCSN applied to the Commission for approval to carry on the activities of a

---

[15] Section 39(4) of the Nigerian Copyright Act] and Reg. 1(1) and (5) [of the CMO Regulations].

[16] Section 39(5) [of the Nigerian Copyright Act].

[17] MCSN was registered on 20 July 1984 with Registration No 64047.

[18] This contract was signed both in Lagos and London on 17 March 1986 and 14 April 1986 respectively.

[19] The grant of exclusive rights is as contained in Article 1(I) of the contract.

[20] See Gervais *Collective Management* 13. In a study conducted for the Department of Canadian Heritage where he noted the different categorizations for collective management organizations.

[21] See An economic analysis of copyright, secondary copyright and collective licensing. Available online at http://www.ipo.gov.uk/ipreview-c4e-sub-plsreport.pdf *Date of use*: 24 March 2012. A report Commissioned by the Copyright Licensing Agency and prepared by PricewaterhouseCoopers LLP (PwC) where three categorizations of a collective management organization was noted as follows: Full voluntary licensing, voluntary licensing with legal backup and legal license.

[22] Section 39(4) Nigerian Copyright Act.

[23] Section 39(5) Nigerian Copyright Act.

collecting society,[24] and after due scrutiny the application was denied.[25] The denial was based on MCSN's refusal[26] to furnish the Commission with requested information.[27] It was also alleged that "the Commission was of the view that the governing structure of MCSN[28] did not place it in a position to represent the full interest of Nigerian creators especially in view of the control that PRS and Mechanical Copyright Protection Society (MCPS) both of London had in MCSN".[29] Unknown to the Commission, the battle line had been drawn. MCSN proceeded to court requesting that the Commission be compelled to approve it as a collecting society.[30] It, however, did not pursue the matter to its logical conclusion but withdrew the matter. This was to be the first in a series of court battles in respect of the approval powers of the Commission as well as its statutory powers and regulatory oversights on collective administration in Nigeria. It should be noted that the challenges was not only between the Commission and the collecting societies, but also between the collecting societies and the user publics.

4.4 Owner, Assignee, or Exclusive Licensee Versus Collecting Society

The Nigerian Copyright Act 1988[31] provided at Section 15[32] that infringement of copyright shall be actionable at the suit of the owners, assignees, or an exclusive licensee. The Nigerian Copyright Act 1988 made no other provisions in respect of collective administration of copyright and related rights, hence organizations

[24] See Okoroji, *Copyright, Neighboring Rights and The New Millionaires* 205 where he stated that "MCSN in a letter dated August 25, 1993, applied to the Nigerian Copyright Council for approval to operate as a collecting society".

[25] Adewopo *Nigerian Copyright System: Principles and Perspectives* 103.

[26] Ibid.

[27] See Okoroji, Op Cit (footnote 24) 205 where he noted that the information which MCSN refused to provide was the membership and financial records of the applicant.

[28] Ibid. The governing council of MCSN had 4 members elected by the general meeting and 4 others nominated by PRS and MCPS. Articles 23(d) of the MCSN's Articles of Association provided that 'no resolution (at any general meeting) shall be deemed to have been carried, whether on a show of hands or on a poll, if the Performing Rights Society or Mechanical Copyright Protection Society has voted against it'.

[29] About a year after the denial of MCSN's application, Performing Mechanical Rights Society (PMRS) was approved to carry on the duties of a collecting society. Approval was given in this regard on 22nd of December 1994.

[30] Musical Copyright Society Nigeria Ltd/Gte V Nigerian Copyright Commission: Suit No: FHC/L/CS/683/94.

[31] The Act has been amended twice and was re-codified in 2004 in the Laws of the Federation of Nigeria at Chapter C28 and is now designated as Nigerian Copyright Act, Cap C28 LFN 2004.

[32] The amendment added a Section 15A and the re-codification rearranged Sections 15 and 15A to now become Sections 16 and 17 of the 2004 Act.

involved in negotiating and granting of licenses as well as collecting and distributing royalties had a free reign with no barriers to the exercise of their rights.[33] The amendments introduced in 1992 and 1999 changed the outlook for the collective administration of copyright and related rights. The unrestricted and unconditional terrain under which collecting societies were free to operate had been truncated by the legal requirement to obtain prior approval to carry on the duties of a collecting society. This sharp twist in policy was to become an issue for judicial elucidation.

In the case of **Musical Copyright Society Nigeria Ltd/Gte v Detail,**[34] an ex-parte order had been obtained by the plaintiff against the defendant for unauthorized use. The defendant raised objections on the ground that the plaintiff lacked *locus standi* to bring the action. The defendant noted that since the plaintiff had provided evidence that it represented more than two million artistes, it was practically performing the functions of a collecting society and therefore required the approval of the Nigerian Copyright Commission to carry on the activities of a collecting society.

The plaintiff denied suing as a collecting society but rather as an owner, assignee, and exclusive licensee as contemplated in Section 15 of the Act.[35] The judge, Odunowo J, considered the attributes of a collecting society in line with the evidence tendered, and noted that copyright owners authorize collecting societies to administer their rights by monitoring use, negotiating and granting licenses, and by collecting and distributing royalties among the owners of such rights. He further noted that copyright owners may come under an umbrella organization or constitute some of their members into a committee that will take up administrative responsibility for royalty collection on behalf of such members instead of each copyright owner suing all infringers individually. The other alternative is for a company to be independently established, as in the instant case, with the primary objective of negotiating with as many copyright owners as possible to secure the assignment of their rights on mutually agreed terms of payment.

Having considered all the evidence, inclusive of the deed of assignments executed with members of the organization which clearly spelt out that the activities to be undertaken were those within the purview of the attributes of a collecting society, the court ruled that

> it is for the foregoing reasons that I have come to the inexorable conclusion, after deep reflection, that the plaintiff is a collecting society. Not having been registered pursuant to Section 32B(4) of the Copyright Act, it cannot be permitted to operate as such body. To do so would be tantamount to subverting not only the letter but also the spirit of the copyright laws of this country.

In a similar case involving the same collecting society, **Musical Copyright Society Nigeria Ltd V Ade Okin Records**[36] the court had to, *inter alia*, consider

---

[33] Compact Disc Technologies V Musical Copyright Society Nigeria Ltd/Gte CA/L/787/2008.

[34] FHC/L/CS/934/95.

[35] Nigerian Copyright Act 1988.

[36] Suit No: FHC/L/CS/216/96.

the meaning of collecting society, the effect of nonapproval and the requirement for *locus standi*. In that particular matter, the plaintiff had brought a motion *ex parte* and obtained an Anton Piller order against the defendant. In a similar reaction as in the *Detail case*, the defendant objected on the grounds that MCSN was not an approved collecting society in accordance with the Nigeria Copyright Act. It was further argued that the order was obtained by fraud as the plaintiff did not disclose its nonapproval status to the court. The plaintiff replied that it sued in its capacity as an owner, assignee, and exclusive licensee and not as a collecting society.

In considering the issues, **Ukeje J** noted that

> the issues that arises therefore is whether the plaintiff/respondent is a collecting society within the meaning of the Section 32B(1) and (2) of the Copyright Act (as inserted by the Copyright (Amendment) Decree 1992 (No.98)

The court then ruled that

> the reading of the deed of assignment, supra, in its entirety, leaves me in no doubt that the plaintiff is a "collecting society".

The court further held that

> based on all the foregoing, I have reached the considered conclusion that the plaintiff herein having not complied with the entire provisions of Section 32B(2) particularly Section 32B(2)d, and consequently, not having been approved as a collecting society by the Copyright Council in terms of Section 32B(2), notwithstanding the plaintiff's apparent compliance with Section 32B(1) and Section 32B(2)(a), (b) and (c) of the Copyright Act, as amended, the plaintiff lacks the locus to institute this suit.

This judgment clarified the fact that an organization representing a large number of right owners and carrying out on their behalf the general duties of negotiating and granting of licenses as well as collecting and distributing royalties to right owners, is a collecting society. The decision also further reinforced the statutory powers of the Commission, namely the fact that without the Commission's prior approval, an organization may not perform the duties of a collecting society[37] and that without the requisite approval, such organizations even though they fall within the purview of owners, assignees, and exclusive licensees would not enjoy the right to institute or maintain an action for copyright infringement.

Dissatisfied with the judgment, MCSN proceeded to the Court of Appeal,[38] raising the under-listed issues for determination:

1. "Whether or not the Appellant as owner, assignee and exclusive licensee of copyright in the musical work allegedly infringed in the action ipso facto have a locus standi to institute and maintain the action by virtue of Section 15(1) of the Copyright Act as amended and the Deed of Assignment (admitted as Exhibit B).

---

37 Section 32B(4) Nigerian Copyright Act.

38 Musical Copyright Society Nigeria Ltd/Gte V Adeokin CA/L/498/97. In the hierarchy of courts in Nigeria, the Court of Appeal is the second highest court next to the Supreme Court.

2. Whether or not a person, (both natural and artificial) particularly a copyright owner must be a collecting Society in order to enjoy the right to enforce the rights attaching to copyright owners, assignees and exclusive licensees properly so called under Section 15 or the Copyright Act, 1988.
3. Whether there is basis for the finding by the learned trial judge that the Appellant is a collecting society for the purpose of determining whether or not it has locus standi or at all.
4. Whether or not the learned trial judge in striking out the Appellant's claim did not derogate from the Appellant's right under Sections 5 and 15 of the Copyright Act, as amended; Section 37 of 1979 constitution; Section 44 of the 1999 Constitution; and Articles 10 and 14 of the African Charter on Human and People's rights enforceable in Nigeria by virtue of Section 12(1) of the 1979 Constitution and 1999 Constitution.
5. Whether or not the provision of Section 15 of the Copyright Act is in conflict with Section 32B or that Section 32B in some material particular do not derogate from the purport and general intendment of copyright legislation in Nigeria.
6. Whether in all the circumstances of this case, the learned trial judge did not abdicate jurisdiction by striking out the Appellant's claim when on the basis of the materials before the Court together with the relevant statutes there was sufficient material for the court, that is, the Federal High Court to assume jurisdiction to hear the Appellant's claim."[39]

It should be noted that the respondents failed to file their brief of argument, hence the appeal was basically predicated on the appellant's brief of argument and issues formulated from the grounds of appeal. Opining on the grounds of appeal, Suleiman Galadima JCA noted that the "grounds of appeal as couched and framed were repetitive, verbose and argumentative with the particulars unnecessarily prolix". He therefore formulated a single issue as follows:

> Whether there is basis for the finding by the learned trial judge that the Appellant is a collecting society for the purpose of determining whether or not it has locus standi at all.[40]

The appeal court noted the reasoning of the lower court, to wit that the appellant had not complied with the entire provisions of Section 32B(2) particularly Section 32(2)(d) and was thus not approved as a collecting society and therefore lacked the locus to institute the suit. He further noted that "it is not in dispute that the appellant commenced the action in its capacity as "owner/Assignee and exclusive licensee of the copyright in the musical work OJUMO RE". After a careful study of "Sections 9, 10 and 15 of the Copyright Act 1989 (then applicable)""[41] the judge held that

---

[39] Ibid at page 2.

[40] Ibid at page 4.

[41] Ibid at page 5.

> the combined effect of all these provisions expressly confer legal rights in copyright to an "owner, assignee or an exclusive licensee of the Copyright[42]

and further held that what was required for *locus standi* in such a matter was that the person claiming to be the copyright owner should fall into any of the categories, namely the author of the work himself; the assignee; the licensee. It is therefore only any of these legally authorized or accredited owners that can seek redress in copyright in the Court of law. Thus, the appellant as owner assignee and exclusive licensee of the Copyright in the allegedly infringed work has legal right and indeed locus standi.[43]

Having addressed the issue of the capacity in which MCSN sued, the question now was whether or not a copyright owner must be a collecting society so as to acquire *locus standi* to enforce his rights as a copyright owner? The definition of a collecting society as stated in Section 32B(8) of the Copyright (Amendment) Act 1992 was considered and it was noted that it was clear that a collecting society is not the same as owner, assignee, and exclusive licensee. The question was then reframed thus:

> whether the locus recognized under the Act is that of a collecting society only so as to justify the court's finding that the Appellant is a collecting society[44]

The court reasoned that by virtue of the interpretation of exclusive licensee as provided in S.39 and the provision of S.15, it was clearly shown that rights are conferred on owners, assignees, and exclusive licensees of copyright works. He noted that

> I cannot find any part of Section 15 or the whole act, where it is stated that the rights are exclusive preserve of collecting society. In the same view, no where in the Appellant's claim has it referred to itself as a collecting society[45]

He therefore opined that there was no basis for considering whether or not the appellant was a collecting society for the purpose of granting it *locus standi* as the issue of collecting society has no relevance to the Appellant's position as secured under Section 15 of the Act. Contrasting his reasoning with that of the trial judge[46] Suleiman Galadima JCA noted:

> I am afraid, the learned trial judge, and I, are totally on different wave lengths on this issue. By striking out the Appellant's claim at this stage, the constitutional right of the Appellant is clearly violated or denied[47]

[42] Ibid.

[43] Ibid at page 5.

[44] Ibid at page 8.

[45] Ibid.

[46] Ukeje J of the Federal High Court (as she then was).

[47] CA/L/498/97 supra at page 9.

He concluded his judgment by concurring with the Appellant's counsel that Section 15A, a further amendment to the Act[48] which came to be after the course of action had taken place would be inapplicable in the determination of the matter. He, however, noted that the right of action vested under Section 15A does not take away the right of action vested under Section 15 of the Act and that even if the amendment effected in 1999 forming Section 15A were to be applied, this still would not affect the appellant's locus as owner, assignee, and exclusive licensee.

> In view of the above, I hold that the 1999 amendment does not apply to this appeal. However, assuming that the Decree applies, the clear position of the Appellant's locus standi as owner assignee and exclusive licensee remains unaffected by the Amendment Decree[49]

This decision clearly rocked the boat as it strengthened the position of MCSN as 'owner, assignee and exclusive licensee'. Like would be expected, this empowered MCSN to take to the streets and administer their rights without the approval of the Commission. This situation brought confusion to the copyright industry. Users who were unwilling to pay capitalized on the nonapproval status of MCSN and made use of works but refused to pay in the guise that they did not know to whom to pay seeing MCSN was not approved, as well as the fact that the approved PMRS had little or no bite in the industry.[50] The resultant effect as captured in the interview[51] referred to at the introduction of this chapter was a situation where right owners were unable to receive royalties and were therefore not remunerated for their creativity.

In a more recent Court of Appeal case, **Compact Disc Technologies Ltd V Musical Copyright Society of Nigeria**[52] delivered on 17 March 2010, the appeal arose from the decision of the lower court[53] where MCSN had obtained judgment as an owner, assignee, or exclusive licensee. The *Adeokin* judgment at the court of

[48] Decree No 42 1999. The section is now Section 17 of the Nigerian Copyright Act 2004. It provides for "Limitation to the right of action" and states that "no action for the infringement of copyright or any right under this Act shall be commenced or maintained by any person-

Carrying on the business of negotiating and granting of licences

Collecting and distributing royalties in respect of copyright works or representing more than fifty owners of copyright in any category of works protected by this Act,

Unless it is approved under Section 39 of this Act to operate as a collecting society or is otherwise issued with a certificate of exemption by the Commission".

[49] This part of the judgment has been held to be an obiter dictum (that is, something said in passing). See Compact Disc Technologies ltd V Musical Copyright Society of Nigeria CA/L/787/2008.

[50] See generally, Shyllon *Intellectual Property Law in Nigeria* 131 where he noted that the "management of silverbird Communications, owners of Rhythm FM station in Lagos had been unable to pay royalty to artist whose records were aired by the station, because it did not know to which collecting body-MCSN or PMRS- such dues should be remitted".

[51] Kolapo and Oduntan 2006-2007-22 Saturday Punch A3.

[52] CA/L/787/2008 delivered on 17th of March 2010.

[53] Federal High Court, Lagos Judicial Division delivered by Honourable Justice J.E. Shakarho on the 5th day August 2008.

appeal had clearly strengthened MCSN's position as owner, assignee, or exclusive licensee. Nonetheless, this appeal was brought challenging the respondent's locus to institute the action as an owner, assignee, or an exclusive licensee of the copyright in compliance with the provisions of Section 15(1) of the copyright Act and not as a collecting society as provided for by Section 32B of the Act. On appeal, the appellants formulated two issues:

(a) "Whether or not an alleged owner, assignee, or exclusive licensee of copyright can validly and solely prosecute a group copyright claim relying on only Section 15(1) of the copyright Act 1988 and the decision of this court in **MSCN LTD V ADEOKIN RECORDS (2007) 13 NWLR 615** to the exclusion of the provision of Sections 15(a) and 32(b) of the copyright Act as amended) 1999.
(b) Whether or not it is a triable issue under Sections 15A and 32 of the 1999 copyright Act (as amended) or—an alleged owner assignee or exclusive licensee to group copyright to ipse dixit plead locus standi without pleading that it has a valid and subsisting collecting society is [sic] license"[54]

Similarly, the respondent raised a total of three issues as follows:

1. "Whether or not the Respondent as owner assignee and exclusive licensee of copyright in the musical work allegedly infringed in the action ipso facto have a locus standi to institute and maintain the action by virtue of Section 15(1) the copyright Act as amended and the Deeds of Assignment executed by different artistes and or Reciprocal Agreements (attached to the Respondent's statement of claim (Formulated from ground 1)
2. Whether or not the Respondent an exclusive Assignee of copyright must be a collecting society and/or have a collecting society's licence in order to be entitled to enforce the right transferred to it by the copyright owners or assignors under the Deeds of Assignment or Reciprocal Agreements. (formulated from Ground 2)
3. Whether the Court of Appeal judgment in the case of Musical Society of Nigeria ltd. Gte V Adeokin Records and Anor (2007) 13 NWLR Part 1952 page 616 delivered on the 27th day of September 2004 was based solely on the Nigerian copyright Act 1988, devoid of the Amendments of 1992 and 1999 (Formulated from Ground 3)."[55]

The court after due consideration of the issues raised by both parties noted that the issues were not mutually exclusive and proceeded to determine the appeal based on the three issues raised in the Respondent's brief.

The respondent argued that by virtue of the provisions of Section 15(1) read in conjunction with the provisions of Sections 9, 10, and 15(1) of the Act, as well as the *Adeokin* case decided at the court of appeal, the respondent's legal right in

[54] CA/L/787/2008 supra at page 5.

[55] Ibid page 6.

copyright as owner, assignee, or exclusive licensee of copyright is settled; hence the provisions of Sections 15A and 32B requiring that approval be obtained are irrelevant. The appellant on the other hand argued that an owner, assignee, or exclusive license may bring a legal action as contemplated by Section 15(1); however, the challenge is that the right to bring such an action is limited by virtue of a statutory condition, a condition precedent to the exercise of such a legal right as provided in Sections 15A and 32B of the Act, to wit, the possession of a collecting society license vide an approval from the Nigerian Copyright Commission. It was therefore its argument that without first meeting the said condition, the respondents lack the requisite jurisdiction to be heard by the court.

The appellant further argued that the *Adeokin* decision was reached based on the law applicable at the time, that is, the Nigerian Copyright Act, 1988 which did not require a copyright owner, assignee, or exclusive licensee to obtain approval and be licensed to operate a collecting society as a condition precedent for instituting or maintaining a legal action under Section 15(1) of the Copyright Act.

The court in considering the arguments, took cognizance of the provisions of Sections 15(1),[56] 15A[57] and 32B[58] and the existing law at the time the cause of action accrued. The learned judge noted that the case at the lower court was filed on 2 August 2007 by which time the existing law was the Copyright Act[59] incorporating both the amendments of 1992 and 1999. The learned judge therefore observed that

> it is rather regrettable with due respect, that the learned trial judge, and indeed the learned counsel to the respective parties, would lose sight of the very obviously fundamental fact that the law applicable, as at 2nd August, 2007 when the action was filed, was the Copyright Act Cap C28 Laws of the Federal Republic of Nigeria, 2004. With due respect, the reference by the learned judge and the learned counsel to the copyright (Amended) Decree 1999 was an unpardonable misnormer.[60]

On the issue of whether or not the respondent is a collecting society or an owner, assignee, exclusive license, the courts appraised the respondent's statement of claim and concluded that although the respondent has not addressed itself as a collecting society, it was without doubt for all intents and purposes, actively involving itself in collecting and distributing royalties in respect of copyright works of the various authors, composers, and organizations for the territory of Nigeria and was therefore a collecting society.

The court further noted that prior to amendment of the 1988 Act, owners, assignees, and exclusive licensees had unrestricted and unconditional legal rights

---

[56] Now Section 16 of the Nigerian Copyright Act 2004.

[57] Now Section 17 of the Nigerian Copyright Act 2004.

[58] Now Section 39 of the Nigerian Copyright Act 2004.

[59] 2004.

[60] CA/L/787/2008 supra at page 12.

to institute actions at the designated court[61] to seek redress for any infringement or violation of their copyright. However, the amendments to the Act had changed the earlier position and now required that the exercise of the hitherto unconditional right of action become conditional.[62]

Opining on the *Adeokin* (court of appeal) case in comparison with the current matter on appeal, the court held that the two cases were most certainly distinguishable from one another in so many ways. First, the *Adeokin case* was decided based on the Nigerian Copyright Act 1988 which had no provision limiting the rights of an owner, assignee, or exclusive licensee. Second, the cause of action arose prior to the amendments to the Act, thus the applicable law was the 1988 copyright Act. On the contrary, the cause of action in this matter arose in 2007 therefore bringing the matter under the purview of the 1992 and 1999 amendments. Third, since the cause of action arose in 2007, a period after all the amendments had been effected, neither the 1988 Copyright Act nor the *Adeokin* case could be applicable to the determination of the instant appeal.

The court decided all three issues in favor of the appellant as follows: On **Issue one** (whether the respondent as owner, assignee, or exclusive licensee can institute an action, based on Section 15(1)) the court resolved in favor of the appellant and held as follows:

> In the light of the above, I have no doubt in my mind that by the combined effect of the provisions of Sections 9, 10, 15(1), 17 and 39 of the copyrights Act, 2004, the respondent ought to have obtained the prior approval of the copyrights commission before instituting the action in the lower court. Thus, having failed to secure or obtain the approval of the copyrights commission prior to the instituting of the action in question, the Respondent lacks the locus standi to institute the action in the lower court.[63]

On **issue two**, (whether or not the respondent as exclusive licensee of copyright must be a collecting society to enforce the rights transferred to it) the Honourable Justice Ibrahim Mohammad Musa Saulawa also held in favor of the appellant as follows:

> I have no doubt in my mind, that the Respondent has been caught up by the web of limitation provision under Section 17 of the copyrights Act, 2004. Having failed to obtain the approval, he is devoid of the necessary locus standi to institute the action in the lower court[64]

On **issue three**, (whether or not the judgment in the case of *MCSN V Adeokin* was based solely on the Copyright Act of 1988, to the exclusion of the 1992 and 1999 amendments) the court distinguishing the *Adeokin case* from the current matter on appeal held that "the MCSN VERSUS ADEOKIN RECORDS' case was

---

[61] The Federal High Court is the designated court for adjudication of Copyright matters in Nigeria. See Section 16(1) of the Nigerian Copyright Act.

[62] In 1992, it was the inclusion of Section 32B now Section 39; whilst in 1999 it was the inclusion of Section 15A now Section 17.

[63] CA/L/787/2008.

[64] Ibid.

decided basically on the earlier copyright Act 1988"[65] prior to the amendments in 1992 and 1999 which introduced the limitations that now represent the current state of the law on collective administration in Nigeria.

The statutory powers of the Commission were reaffirmed in all the cases listed above save for the *Adeokin* appeal case which has been clearly distinguished in the *Compact Disc Technology case*. These cases clarified the fact that MCSN or indeed any other owner, assignee, and exclusive licensee prior to the amendments in 1992 and 1999 had unconditional and unrestricted rights to institute or maintain an action for infringement of copyright. However, the introduction of the amendments in 1992 and 1999 has placed a limitation on the erstwhile unconditional and unrestricted right of the owner, assignee, or exclusive licensee to wit that they must now obtain the approval of the Commission evidenced by the issuance of a license to operate as a collecting society, prior to instituting any infringement proceedings.

Notwithstanding the above, the powers of the Commission have once again, in an ironical twist, been challenged and questioned. In one of the very recent judgments[66] on collective administration in Nigeria, **Musical Copyright Society of Nigeria Limited V Nigerian Copyright Commission,**[67] The plaintiffs/applicants sought for the enforcement of their fundamental rights, praying for a declaration that "the continued threats of detention, harassment and intimidation by the respondents is unlawful, unwarranted and in breach of their fundamental rights"[68] They noted that sometime in May 1999, the first respondent and its agents invaded the offices of the Applicants and seized several files, documents, and working instruments of the First Applicant and took away an officer of the first applicant without warrant or arrest. It was further noted that "sometime in May 2007, the respondent issued a public statement aimed at further attacking and infringing the fundamental rights of the 1st Applicant to freedom to own property and to engage in lawful economic activities calling on the public not to deal with or engage in business with the 1st Applicant"[69] The Applicants also noted that on 14 December 2007, about 20 fully armed mobile policemen stormed the business premises of the First Applicant and harassed, intimidated, rough-handled, manhandled, and held everybody within the premises hostage for more than 2 hours.[70] Two officers of the First Applicant were later arrested and detained at the office of the First Respondent where there was "little or no ventilation and with no lighting or power supply"[71] All this while, it was also noted that there was no order of

[65] Ibid.

[66] The ruling was made on the 25th July 2011.

[67] FHC/L/CS/35/2008.

[68] Ibid at page 2.

[69] Ibid at page 7.

[70] Ibid.

[71] Ibid.

court, warrant of arrest, or search shown to or served on the Second and Fifth Applicants or other officers of the First Applicant.[72]

Responding, the First Respondent referred to Paragraph 10 of its Counter Affidavit averring on its powers to enforce the Copyright Act inclusive of powers to enter into any premises without warrant, inspect and seize any document or contrivance relating to piracy, arrest and prosecute any suspect and generally exercise all powers, rights, and privileges of a Police Officer in the investigation and prosecution of copyright crime.[73] The respondent further noted that "the International Federation of Phonographic Industries (IFPI) wrote a petition to the 1st Respondent complaining that the 1st Applicant is illegally infringing on the right of its members by authorizing the reproduction of musical and film works of its members without permission"[74] and that in the course of carrying out investigations it was discovered that the First Applicant indeed authorized the reproduction of several foreign musical and film works.[75] After considering the submissions of both parties, the Judge noted that

> the phrase "the right and privileges of a Police Officer" is a peculiar one. Not all acts of infringement amount to privacy [sic]. And charging unwarranted into premises on the Complaint of a supposed owner or licensee of a Copyright is illegal and unconstitutional. No police men has [sic] such "right or privileges".[76]

The judge was of the opinion that the several arrests and seizures made by the Commission on the First Applicant and its premises could not reasonably be considered as actions done to detect and prevent crime. He noted that the rights in respect of the complaint lodged by IFPI had not been adjudicated upon; and that the works over which the claims were based were not detailed.[77] The learned judge therefore held that

> the arrests and seizures were arbitrary and heavy landed [sic]; the actions were those of an agency determined to bring to heal an offensive, rather than an offending body corporate and its executive officers. The 1st respondent has failed to acknowledge, appreciate or welcome the notion and the reality that owners and assignees of copyright can enforce property rights without necessarily being registered as collecting societies by the Copyright Commission. Registration as a collecting society is not a prerequisite for the enjoyment and exercise of the rights of an owner or exclusive licensee of Copyright.[78]

This judgment is clearly not in tandem with the *Compact Disc Technology* (court of appeal) case. Although the doctrine of judicial precedents[79] and the principle of

---

[72] Ibid at page 8.

[73] Ibid at page 12.

[74] Ibid at page 13.

[75] Ibid.

[76] Ibid at page 15.

[77] Ibid.

[78] Ibid at page 16.

[79] See http://www.lawteacher.net/PDF/Judicial%20Precedent.pdf *Date of use*: 5 May 2012 where Asif Tufal noted that judicial precedent means the process whereby judges follow previously decided cases where the facts are of sufficient similarity.

stare decisis[80] encourages that earlier decision be followed, the learned justice, Charles Efanga Archibong did not rely on the current court of appeal case (*Compact Disc Technology*) but rather relied on the *Adeokin* appeal case, a case which was predicated on the Nigerian Copyright Act 1988—an act which had been amended twice and had changed the position of the law with regard to rights to institute and maintain an action for infringement of copyright by owners, assignees, and exclusive licensees' of copyright and related rights. This judgment appears to have left some food for thought to the Nigerian Copyright Commission particularly when it noted that the Copyright Commission and its principal officers should not be in the business of subverting the property rights of copyright owners.[81] This is the current status on the judicial plateau, but as would be imagined, the Nigerian Copyright Commission has appealed the decision[82] but the appeal is yet to be heard.

4.5 Power to Not Approve

The amendments to the Nigerian Copyright Act giving the Nigerian Copyright Commission *inter alia* statutory and regulatory oversights on collecting societies within the general framework of copyright and related rights collective administration in Nigeria provide for both positive and negative powers. Positive in the sense that it empowers the Nigerian Copyright Commission to "approve", in other words granting the Nigerian Copyright Commission powers to authorize the doing of certain things; and negative in that it also empowered the Nigerian Copyright Commission "to not approve", that is it gave it powers to restrain, debar, stop, and limit the ability to do certain things.[83]

Section 39(2)[84] gives the Nigerian Copyright Commission a discretion to approve a society on certain grounds. The wording of that section states that "The Commission *may approve* a society" if it is satisfied about the fulfillment of certain conditions. The use of the word "may" clearly denotes the discretionary nature of the powers granted the Commission. Subsection 3 of the same section gives the Commission the power *to not approve*. It provides that "the Commission shall not approve another society in respect of any class of copyright owners", if it is satisfied about certain matters. This time the wording of that particular section uses the word "shall"

---

80 Ibid. Where it was noted that the doctrine of judicial precedent involves an application of the principle of *stare decisis* that is, to stand by the decided. In practice, this means that inferior courts are bound to apply the legal principles set down by superior courts in earlier cases. This provides consistency and predictability in the law.

81 FHC/L/CS/35/2008 Op Cit at footnote 67.

82 *Nigerian Copyright Commission V Musical Copyright Society Nigeria Ltd/Gte* CA/L/925/2011.

83 See generally, Veljko *Positive and Negative Power* 1 where it was noted that they are "two closely related poles of the same power cycle".

84 Nigerian Copyright Act 2004.

but then also uses the words "if it is satisfied". The use of the word "shall" connotes that the Commission is to perform a mandatory duty but the use of the words "if it is satisfied" provides for the exercise of the Commission's discretion in the determination of what is to be done. The CMO regulation which gives effect to the provisions of the Nigerian Copyright Act,[85] provides that Subject to the provisions of the Regulation, "a licence shall be valid for 3 years and may be renewed every 2 years, in accordance with the procedure herein stipulated".[86] The regulation goes further to provide for the Commission to "refuse to approve an application for renewal of a licence if it is of the opinion that the collective management organisation, no longer meets the requirements for grant of licence".[87] The *Detail*, *Adeokin*, and *Compact Disc* cases all threw some light on the challenges in collective administration as it concerns the positive powers, that is, the powers of the Commission to approve a collecting society. Yet on the other side of the pool as noted by Veljko is the negative power to not approve. This power has been exercised four times by the Commission: the first time was when the Nigerian Copyright Commission did not approve the application made by MCSN for a license to operate as a collecting society immediately after the issuance of the Copyright (collecting societies) regulation 1993.[88] The second time was when a nonrenewal of approval was conveyed to the PMRS in respect of its application for renewal of its license.[89] The most recent exercise of this negative power records the third and fourth instances, when in 2010[90] the Commission once again declined the application by MCSN[91] and Wireless Application Service Providers (WASP) for approval to operate as a collective management organization. At about that time, a new regulation on collective administration had been issued and the earlier one was repealed. This regulation was the result of a strategic reform of collective administration in Nigeria which eventually culminated in the call for indication of interest[92] to operate a collective management organization and eventually the actual invitation for applications[93] for approval to operate as a

[85] Section 39(7) of the Nigerian Copyright Act provides that "The Commission shall have power to make regulations specifying the conditions necessary to give effect to" the purposes of this section of this Act.

[86] Regulation 1(9) CMO Regulation.

[87] Reg 3(3) CMO Regulation. The repealed Copyright (Collecting Societies) Regulation 1993 had a similar provision at regulation 16 of that regulation.

[88] See Okoroji, *Copyright Neighboring Rights and the new Millionaires* 200 where he noted that MCSN applied on 25 August 1993 but the application was declined.

[89] The nonrenewal of the application by PMRS was conveyed to them on 22 December 2006 vide a letter referenced NCC/ADM.205/T45.

[90] The letter of denial was issued to MCSN on the 20th May, 2010 vide a letter referenced NCC/ADM.515/II/451.

[91] The application was dated 1st July 2009.

[92] Public Notice issued by the Nigerian Copyright Commission in the Guardian Newspaper of, Monday, December 29th, 2008.

[93] Applications were called for vide a public notice issued by the Nigerian Copyright Commission in the Guardian Newspaper of Wednesday, June 24th, 2009.

collective management organization. MCSN was one of the three applicants[94]; unfortunately, its application and that of WASP were denied.

In the exercise of the negative powers—the "not to approve powers"—the Nigerian Copyright Commission was challenged when it gave a nonrenewal of approval to operate as a collecting society to PMRS. PMRS sought the relief of the court[95] via an order of *certiorari* that the decision of the Nigerian Copyright Commission to not approve its renewal be quashed. It further sought an order of *mandamus* directing that the Nigerian Copyright Commission be directed to issue a letter/certificate of renewal of approval to PMRS. In addressing the relief sought, the court distilled three issues requiring to be dealt with. Of interest for present purposes is the third issue, namely the question whether the Applicant was entitled to the orders of *certiorari* and *mandamus* prayed for in the application. The applicants argued and submitted that a writ of *certiorari* lies to remove proceedings from an inferior tribunal or court to a superior court to be quashed for excess of jurisdiction. The respondent on the other hand argued that a writ of *certiorari* can only be against bodies exercising judicial or quasi-judicial authority and in respect of acts performed in that capacity and not against administrative or executive actions.[96] As to the *mandamus*, he noted that the applicants had not satisfied the conditions precedent to the grant of the renewal as stipulated in Section 39(2) of the Nigerian Copyright Act and that an "order of mandamus is always granted when a public officer has a duty to perform a particular function mandatorily but not where the performance of that act or function lies within his discretion."[97] He therefore submitted that by virtue of Section 39(2) of the Nigerian Copyright Act, the First Respondent had discretion to approve or not approve the application for renewal and in such a situation, it would be inappropriate to grant a writ of *mandamus* to compel the First Respondent to exercise his direction in any particular way.[98]

In arriving at a decision, the learned judge noted that the act complained of was a mere administrative act and an order of *certiorari* would not lie against such an act. He therefore held that there was no basis for the issuance of the writ of *certiorari*. On the *mandamus*, the learned judge held that Section 39(2) gives the First Respondent discretionary approval powers over collecting societies. He therefore held as follows:

> it is trite that this will not be acceded to where what the order is directed at is the exercise of the discretionary power of the respondent, as in this case... In that sense since the grant of approval lies within the discretion of the 1st respondent, a writ of Mandamus cannot issue to compel him to do that which is at his discretion[99]

---

[94] The other applicants were Copyright Society of Nigeria (COSON) and Wireless Application Service Providers (WASP).

[95] Performing Mechanical Rights Society Ltd/Gte V Nigerian Copyright Commission: Suit No: FHC/L/CS/61/2007 delivered by Justice A.O. Ajakaiye on the 4th June 2009.

[96] The learned counsel to the First Respondent referred to the case of *Prof Nwaoboshi and* 4 *ors V The Military Governor of Delta State and* 2 *Ors* (2003) 11 NWLR (Part 831) 305 at 310.

[97] FHC/L/CS/61/2007.

[98] This position will find support in the case of Layanju V Araoye (1959) SC NLR 416.

[99] FHC/L/CS/61/2007.

Both prayers—for *Certiorari* and *Mandamus*—were therefore refused for lack of merit and the suit was accordingly struck out.

4.6 Constitutionality of Sections 17 and 39 of the Nigerian Copyright Act

The Constitution of the Federal Republic of Nigeria[100] guarantees the Fundamental Human Rights of every citizen as prescribed by the Universal Declaration of Human Rights[101] and the African Charter for Human and People's Rights.[102] One of the fundamental rights guaranteed by these instruments is the right to own property.[103] In the controversy of collecting societies in Nigeria, the issue of constitutionality of Sections 17 and 39 vis a vis the right to freedom to own property has been contested in the courts. In *Musical Copyright Society of Nigeria Ltd/Gte (Applicants) Versus Nigerian Copyright Commission* (Respondents),[104] the applicants sought the following relief:

1. "A declaration that Sections 17 and 39 of the Copyright Act 2004 are unconstitutional in so far as they circumscribe the Applicant's Fundamental Right as guaranteed under Sections 40 and 44 of the 1999 Constitution.
2. A Declaration that the Applicant has a right as owner, assignee, and exclusive licensee of various authors and entities to exploit and enjoy her properties in the works and that these rights ought not to be abrogated, disturbed, or frustrated except by just laws which offer just compensation and are in accord with Section 44 of the constitution of the Federal Republic of Nigeria.
3. A declaration that Section 17 and Section 39 (formerly Section 15A and Section 32B) of the copyright Act 2004 are unconstitutional null and void in so far as they seek to abrogate rights of property that have been accrued before the promulgation of the said sections of the Copyright Act.
4. A Declaration that the Applicant does not require a license from the Respondent in order to carry on their business in the exploitation of rights validly and legitimately required by the Applicant.

[100] Cap C.23 Laws of the Federation of Nigeria 2004 at this chapter (hereinafter referred to as The Nigerian Constitution).

[101] *Adopted and proclaimed by General Assembly resolution* 217 *A (III) of* 10 *December* 1948 (hereinafter referred to as *The UN Charter).*

[102] (Adopted 27 June 1981, OAU Doc. CAB/LEG/67/3 rev. 5, 21 I.L.M. 58 (1982), entered into force 21 October 1986) (hereinafter referred to as the African Charter).

[103] The Nigerian Constitution provides for it at Sections 43 and 44, whilst the UN charter provides for it at Article 17 and that of the African Charter at Article 14.

[104] Suit No: FHC/L/CS/478/2008 Before the Honorable Justice I.M Sani on the 3rd of April 2009.

5. A declaration that Sections 17 and Section 39 of the Copyright Act 2004 are contrary to the provisions of Articles 10, and 14 of the African Charter on Human and People's Right Ratification and Enforcement Act Cap A9 Laws of the Federation 2004 made enforceable by Section 12(1) of the 1999 constitution of the Federal Republic of Nigeria 1999
6. And for any further or other orders as the Honorable Court may deem fit to make in the circumstances[105]"

Four issues were distilled as follows:

1. "Does the applicants [sic] have property?
2. Does the Applicant have a constitutional right to property
3. Is the Respondent's action impeding the enjoyment of that property, if they have one?
4. Is there a lawful justification for the action of the Respondents?[106]"

Arguing on the issues raised, the learned counsel for the applicant referred to the reciprocal agreements with international bodies, legal text on copyright,[107] judicial decisions,[108] and public notices issued by the respondents not to deal with the applicant because the applicant is not licensed by the Respondent. Reference was also made to Section 44 of the Constitution which makes provision for the prohibition of compulsory acquisition of property and Article 14 of the African Charter, which guarantees the right to property. The learned counsel therefore contended that by virtue of the rights acquired through the reciprocal agreements ever since 1984, a subsequent enactment or legislation could not abrogate rights that had been acquired prior to the enactment except by express and unequivocal provisions. He referred the court to the *Adeokin*[109] court of appeal case and Section 52(3) of the Nigerian Copyright Act, Schedule 5 2004 (the transitional and saving provisions in the fifth schedule), and further contended that by the combined effect of the decision and enactment, the Copyright Act cannot affect the right the applicant had acquired. He therefore concluded that the acts of the respondent were impeding the enjoyment of the Applicant's right to property and urged the court to hold Sections 17 and 39 of the Copyright Act unconstitutional.

The learned counsel for the Respondent was of the opinion that all the five prayers by the applicants were anchored on one major issue, to wit, that Sections 17 and 39 of the Nigerian Copyright Act violated Applicant's Fundamental Rights as guaranteed by

---

[105] Ibid.

[106] Ibid.

[107] See *Musical Copyright Society of Nigeria Ltd/Gte V Nigerian Copyright Commission* Suit No. FHC/L/CS/478/2008 at p4 where reference was made to "Copengha and Scon Janes on Copy Rights [sic], Published by Sweet and Maxwell". The author is convinced that the work referred to by the court was that of Copinger and Skone-James.

[108] *Nafiu Rabiu Versus The State* (1981) 2 NCLR P. 293 at 362 and *Agbakoba Versus. Director SSS* (1984) 6 NWLR PT.351 P. 475 at 499-500.

[109] 2007 (13) NWLR PT. 1052 P. 616 at 631-632.

the Nigerian Constitution. Learned counsel contended as to whether Respondent could challenge the provisions of the Act under a fundamental rights application noting that by virtue of Order 2(1) of the Fundamental Right (Enforcement Procedure), the operative word is "infringement", which has to be a physical act. He further contended that Sections 17 and 39 did not restrict the right of Copyright owners to associate or assemble but gave the Respondent power to approve collecting societies and make it an offence to operate without approval. He referred the court to Section 45 which provides for restriction on and derogation from fundamental human rights as well as the case of *Medical and Health Workers Union of Nig V Honorable Minister of Labour and Productivity,*[110] where it was held that Sections 3 and 5 of the Trade Union Act, which provides the conditions to be met by an applicant before it can be registered as a trade union, are not inconsistent with the provisions of the 1999 constitution.

On the issue of the right to property guaranteed under Section 44, learned counsel for the respondent noted that the section dealt with compulsory acquisition whereas Sections 17 and 39 had nothing to do with compulsory acquisitions as they relate to applicant's property. The sections rather describe the activities of a collecting society and provide the conditions to be fulfilled by an organisation desirous of carrying out the said activities of a collecting society. Learned counsel therefore concluded that considering the evidence tendered and applicant's affidavit, it was without doubt that the applicant was a collecting society and therefore required the Respondent's approval.

On the prayer that Section 17 and Section 39 of the Copyright Act 2004 were contrary to the provisions of Articles 10 and 14 of the African Charter on Human and People's Right, the learned counsel to the respondent noted that the Constitution was the ground norm and as such the Articles from the African Charter on Human and People's rights could not grant rights beyond what the constitution had provided. He therefore urged the court to hold that Sections 17 and 39 did not violate articles 10 and 14 of the African Charter. Counsel drew the attention of the court to Section 38 of the Nigerian Copyright Act, which gives the Respondent powers to enforce the Copyright Act and that such powers were not limited to works acquired before or after the laws were passed. He noted that Section 39 of the Nigerian Copyright Act regulates the business of Collecting societies and not the rights that may have passed subsequent or prior to the commencement of the law. He therefore submitted that anyone desirous of carrying out the functions of a collecting society requires a license in accordance with Section 39 of the Nigerian Copyright Act, which section could not be said to have retrospective effect.

After a careful review of the submission, the court's assessment of the fundamental question was that it had to do with whether the provisions of Sections 17 and 39 of the Nigerian Copyright Act circumscribed the Applicant's Fundamental Rights as guaranteed under Sections 40 and 44 of the Nigerian Constitution. In addressing this fundamental question another question emerged: "Does the

---

110 (2005) 17 NWLR PT.953 P. 120 at 155.

requirement to obtain a licence from the respondent to operate amounts to compulsory acquisition of property or right?"

The judge noted that the requirement by the law for a party to fulfill certain conditions before he becomes entitled to the exercise of his rights could not be tantamount to compulsory acquisition of that right or property.[111] He therefore held that the mere fact that the applicant was required to obtain a licence before it could carry on business was not the same as compulsory acquisition of applicant's rights and thus no right of the applicant had been breached under Section 44 of the 1999 constitution. The action therefore failed and was accordingly dismissed.

4.7 The Commission's Single Society Policy: Monopoly Versus Liberalization

4.7.1 Introduction

The right which creators obtain upon creating a work is a virtual monopoly to the exclusion of all others to restrain any and everyone from exploiting the creator's work without prior authorization having been obtained. This monopolistic attribute of copyright appears to have been extended to the collective administration of copyright and it has been opined that since copyright is vested in authors and collective management organizations administer these rights, they should be allowed to freely associate and exploit their collective rights.[112] The exploitation of these collective rights are best achieved when a collecting society is able to aggregate the rights within a particular category of work. This aggregation, often referred to as "world repertoire" is often achieved by legislative means or by the "voluntary union of all national and foreign rightholders, thereby leading to a de facto monopoly position"[113]. On the other hand is the school of thought

[111] See Regina Obiageli Nwodo's concurring views with that of the lead judgment in the Compact Disc Case where she opined on condition precedents to the exercise of a right and said, "the right or competence to institute proceedings in a court of law for redress or assertion of a right enforceable at law is not unlimited… where there is a statutory provision from where such a right enures, the conditions precedent to the exercise of that right becomes a limitation to the direct access to court… therefore compliance with this condition precedent to the institution of an action by any person carrying on the business of negotiating and granting of license or persons collecting and distributing royalties in respect of copyright works is fundamental to the competency of the action and the court to proceed with the suit... Section 17 does not oust the subject matter jurisdiction of the court or **derogation from the rights of citizen, it only postpones the time for instituting a suit which means go and comply to the provision and get back to the court"**.

[112] See generally Josef Drexl *Collecting Societies and Competition* 15 Available online at http://193.174.132.100/shared/data/pdf/drexl_-_crmos_and_competition.pdf *Date of use*: 31 March 2012.

[113] Uchtenhagen *The Setting-up of New Copyright Societies* 5.

postulating the imperatives and advantages of competition and how it encourages its players to compete to achieve the same goal, thus triggering what otherwise would not have happened as things get done faster, cheaper, and better.[114] This school of thought believes that "as a monopoly, copyright vests copyright owners with an easy, government-created ability to act in anti-competitive and anti-innovative ways, ways that are harmful to the public interest".[115] It also believes that in view of the public interest concerns, there is an obligation on government to exercise anti-trust oversights[116] over collective management organizations. This is believed to be important as the pro-single collecting society system instituted by the amendments to the Nigerian Copyright Act is considered to be "antithetical to the emerging global and regulatory trends which is consistently in the direction of competition and liberalization".[117]

4.7.2 Legal and Regulatory Framework

Prior to the enactment of legal provisions on collective administration in Nigeria, a consultant to the World Intellectual Property Organisation (WIPO), Dr Ulrich Uchtenhagen[118] was in Nigeria on a special mission to study the collective administration terrain in Nigeria in order to report on his findings. The mission which began on the 12th of May 1991 lasted for nine (9) days. During this period, the consultant visited several Nigerian artistes[119] and met with several government offices[120] and top government functionaries.[121] In his report he noted that if the Nigerian music industry was not pragmatic, it would end up with several collecting societies, none of which would collect anything. He therefore recommended a single collecting society structure for Nigeria, further noting that multiple collecting societies had rarely succeeded in developing countries.[122]

[114] See Boldrin and Levine *Against Intellectual monopoly* 124.

[115] Patry Moral Panics 101.

[116] See Adewopo *Nigerian Copyright System: Principles and Perspectives* 89 where he noted that "This becomes more important in the case of the developing countries, where anti-trust laws are frequently inadequately codified or not suited to the kind of activities undertaken by collecting societies, as distinguished from activities of producing or trading enterprises".

[117] Adewopo *Proposals for Liberalisation of Collecting Societies in Nigeria* 132.

[118] Dr. Uchtenhagen was the former Director General of SUISA, the Swiss Collecting Society.

[119] See Okoroji *Copyright, Neigbouring Rights and the New Millionaires* 199 where the names of Victor Olaiya, Christy Essien Igbokwe and Onyeka Onwenu were mentioned.

[120] Ibid. He met with the biggest broadcasting stations, Federal Radio Commission of Nigeria (FRCN), the Nigerian Television Authority (NTA) and the Nigerian Copyright Council as it was called at the time/(NCC).

[121] Ibid. He met with the Minister of Culture and Social Welfare as well as the Minister in charge of Trade and Tourism.

[122] Ibid.

The legal and regulatory framework for collective administration in Nigeria is aptly captured in the Nigerian Copyright Act[123] and the Copyright (Collective Management Organization Regulations)[124] as follows:

> **Section 39(1)** A Collecting Society (in this section referred to as "a society") may be formed in respect of anyone or more rights of copyrights owners for the benefit of such owners, and the society may apply to the Commission for approval to operate as a collecting society for the purpose of this Act.

This subsection provides the legislative backing for a single society to administer multiple rights of multiple works. It provides that a single society may be formed for the purpose of administering any one or more rights of copyright owners and for the benefit of such owners. Section 1 of the Nigerian Copyright Act provides for works eligible for copyright and lists out six of them,[125] while Sections 6–9 provide for the rights that accrue to such works.[126] In an illustrative form, Section 39(1) provides that society "A" may be formed to administer the performing rights[127] as well as recording (mechanical) rights[128] of Mr. Bandele's musical and sound recording works for his benefits. Furthermore, Section 39(3) provides the following:

> The Commission shall not approve another society in respect of any class of copyright owners, if it is satisfied that an existing approved society adequately protects the interest of that class of copyright owners

---

[123] Cap C28 LFN 2004.

[124] Published in the official gazette as GN No. 67 vol 94 3rd October 2007.

[125] Literary; musical; artistic; cinematograph films; sound recordings; and broadcasts.

[126] In the case of **literary and musical** works: Rights to (1) reproduce; (2) publish; (3) perform; (4) translate[produce, reproduce, perform or publish]; (5) Make a cinematograph film or a record in respect of the work; (6) distribute; (7) broadcast or communicate to the public; (8) adaptation; and (9) In relation to adaptation or translation (all the rights in 1–7). In all there are 8 basic rights.

In the case of **artistic works**: Rights to (1) Reproduce; (2) Publish; (3) Include the work in any cinematograph film; (4) make an adaptation; and (5) In relation to an adaptation, any of the rights specified in 1–3. In all there are 4 basic rights.

In the case of **cinematograph film**: Rights to (1) make a copy (reproduce); (2) Broadcast or communication to the Public; (3) make any record embodying the recording in any part of the soundtrack associated with the film by utilizing such soundtrack; and (4) distribute. In all there are 4 basic rights.

In the case of **Sound Recording**: Rights to (1) direct or indirect reproduction; (2) broadcasting; (3) communication to the public; and (4) distribution. In all there are 4 basic rights.

In the case of **Broadcast:** Right to (1) Record; (2) Re-broadcast of a broadcast; (3) Communication to the public of a television broadcast; and (4) Distribution to the public. In all there are 4 basic rights.

[127] Performing rights refer to the right of the copyright owner to authorize performance of the work in public. See Section 6(1)a(iii) of the Nigerian Copyright Act.

[128] Mechanical rights refer to the right of the copyright owner to authorize reproduction of the work in any material form. See Section 6(1)a(1) of the Nigerian Copyright Act.

This subsection introduced the term "class of copyright owners' and apparently, no explanation or interpretation of the phrase or the words in the phrase is provided. The earlier parts of the act used words such as **works**, (for instance works eligible for copyright,[129] literary works[130] etc.;) and **rights**, (for instance "the exclusive right to control..[131], shall include the right to…[132];) but the sudden introduction of **class of copyright owners** at this section without any interpretation creates a gap in this respect and leaves the responsibility of interpretation to the individual reader, and one may have to imagine that "a class of copyright owner" may refer to what the act contemplated in Section 1, that is, the class of literary, musical, artistic, cinematograph films, sound recording and broadcast copyright owners'. It could also be argued that "class of copyright owners" could mean what the act provides for at Sections 6–9, that is, class of copyright owners who hold rights of reproduction, performance, publication, distribution, communication to the public, broadcast, translation, and adaptation. The first scenario has a broader perspective, in that each class of work has embedded in it several rights. It may then be an option to work with the assumption that the drafter's intent was that "class of copyright owners" was to be read in accordance with the works listed at Section 1. It must however be noted that the operations of collecting societies vary from one country to the other. While some adopt a work-based approach[133] others adopt a right based approach in respect of their operations..[134] As observed at Sections 6–9 of the Nigerian Copyright Act, copyright owners enjoy several rights based on each work. The literary and musical copyright owners enjoy at least eight distinct rights[135] under the Nigerian Copyright Act, while the artistic copyright owners enjoy about four basic rights.[136]

Taking cognizance of the two possibilities, the first paints a picture where one can say, Section 39(3) therefore intends that two collecting societies shall not exist at the same time in respect of the same class of copyright owners. Illustratively, Society B cannot obtain the Commission's approval to administer Musical works when the Commission is satisfied that Society A adequately protects the interest of Musical copyright owners. In other words, this subsection is pro-single society as against multiple societies in respect of the same work. Using the second scenario, Section 39(3) could also mean two societies shall not be approved by the

[129] Section 1.

[130] Section 1(1)a.

[131] Sections 6(1)a; 7(1); 8(1).

[132] Section 8(2).

[133] Nigeria for instance grants licenses to collecting societies based on works and not rights. I however note that all rights are derived from works but notwithstanding licenses could be granted based on works or rights and Nigeria so far as granted based on works alone. The Copyright Society of Nigeria is licensed for Musical Works and Sound Recording, while the Reproduction Rights Organisation of Nigeria (REPRONIG) is licensed for literary works.

[134] Gervais *Collective Management* 26.

[135] Section 6(1)a.

[136] Section 6(1)b.

Commission to administer the same rights of copyright owners. Illustratively, Society B will not be approved by the Commission to administer the performing rights of copyright owners when the Commission is satisfied that society A adequately protects the interest of performing rights owners. Whatever interpretation is adopted, one thing is clear: the subsection appears to be pro-single society and possibly anti-multiple collecting society, seeing that the Commission will not grant approval to two collecting societies to administer either the same work or the same right during the same period once it is satisfied that the existing one adequately protects the interests of right owners. The debate however becomes heated when the Commission becomes dissatisfied with the existing collecting society. This was the situation in 2005 when the Nigerian Copyright Commission granted approval to MCSN when PMRS was the existing (approved) collecting society. In a position paper prepared by the Commission,[137] the rationale for approving a second society while the existing one was still operating was enunciated as follows:

> The Commission is not satisfied that PMRS alone adequately represents or protects the interest of copyright owners, authors, and composers in the music industry. Consequently, the Commission has decided and hereby approves MCSN as the second collecting society for music to administer the rights of its members. The approval is in accordance with the provisions of Section 32B of the Copyright Act as amended and the Regulation of 1992. The Commission has given due regard to the legitimate expectation of our large population of authors, composers, and artistes who are entitled to earn income from their creative enterprise. It is important to bear in mind that the Commission's decision should be considered in the best interest of the large community of owners of copyright and neighboring right whose music has been extensively exploited without any representation and not as a victory or defeat for any section or interest in the industry. The approval of MCSN is not in principle at variance with the commonly held view for a single collecting society for rights in music in Nigeria. However, the Commission believes that a single society structure cannot be arbitrarily imposed especially in the present circumstance, but can only be attained in time as industry-driven and by right owners themselves as a genuine demonstration of their commitment to a viable collective administration system and in pursuance of their right to self-determination.[138]

The aforementioned license granted to the MCSN was the first and up to now the only time when the discretion granted the Commission in Section 39(3) ("if it is satisfied") was exercised in a positive form.[139] As indicated above, that subsection also contemplates a negative exercise of the power by "not approving".[140] In this instance ,however, the exercise of the discretion was a positive one, approving the application of MCSN as the second collecting society for music.

---

137 The unpublished paper is titled "Collective Administration in the Music Industry" The paper was prepared to provide the rationale for the approval of a second collecting society for Music in Nigeria. Dated 6th May 2005 (The same day MCSN was approved).

138 Ibid.

139 The certificate of Approval was dated 6 May 2005.

140 With respect to "negative and positive powers please see my earlier comments at para. 4.4 above "Powers to Not approve".

The license lasted for only six months[141] due to a subsequent nullification of the approval granted.[142] This example, in my view shows that the Commission may not altogether be anti-multiple collecting societies but rather is guided by the need to protect the public interest and ensure that on a case-by-case basis, issues are considered in line with international best practices, while at the same time taking cognizance of nationalistic interests against the backdrop of the national level of development.

Beyond statutory imperative, the Nigerian Copyright Commission's pro-single collective management organization policy was based on several motivations inclusive of the level of development of the user public, the per capital income of the average citizen and several other issues which after the Commission thought about, culminated in a position paper on the subject matter as follows:

1. The need to avoid confusion in the licensing environment that would arise where more than one organization is approved to licence users in respect of the same category of works.
2. The need to ensure that users of copyright works have a simple and uncomplicated access to works they require.
3. Where several organizations exist managing the same rights, it is always difficult to make precise demarcation of the scope of their authorized management and repertoire.
4. The existence of more than one organization in a particular sphere of collection increases cost of administration and reduces the royalty available for distribution to authors of works.
5. Previous experimentation with multiple collective management model resulted in unending acrimony and rivalry resulting in lack of focus and nonperformance by either of the organizations.
6. The existence of more than one organization for the same category of rights will invariably lead to users rejecting to pay to any of the organizations, as they may not want to be exposed to legal liability by the second organization.
7. A cursory examination of what obtains in the field of collective management of copyright internationally shows a preponderance of the single society model particularly in developing countries…
8. The Commission's Policy also takes cognizance of the official position of the World Intellectual Property Organization (***WIPO—the United Nations Specialized Agency for Intellectual Property***) which recommends the establishment of a single society for each category of works or class of rights in a given country.[143]

[141] The approval was withdrawn on the 18th November 2005 vide a memo NCC/ADM.364/T/33.

[142] The letter stated that "the President of the Federal Republic of Nigeria… has directed the nullification of the approval granted to your organization. Accordingly, the certificate earlier issued is hereby withdrawn".

[143] Nigerian Copyright Commission's Position Paper to the Honorable Attorney General of the Federation and Minister of Justice dated August 16, 2010.

4.7.3 Conclusion

The powers of the Nigerian Copyright Commission to approve and to not approve have been the major subject of discussion in this chapter and an attempt was made to highlight some of the challenges that have been brought to the fore by reason of the exercise of these powers. The concurring judgment[144] of Regina Obiageli Nwodo in the *Compact Disc Case*[145] noted that Section 17 of the Nigerian Copyright Act does not oust the jurisdiction of the court in respect of the subject matter or derogate from the rights of citizens, but only postpones the time for instituting a suit, which means that citizens need to first go and comply with the provision, after which they can come back to the court.[146]

The pro-single or anti-multiple slant of the Act is apparent. This appears even more so in light of the recommendation made by the WIPO consultant, Dr Ulrich Uchtenhagen, which pointed the country in the direction of a single collecting society structure and thus can be seen to have influenced the legislation in this regard. The attempt to introduce a second collecting society for music in Nigeria through the approval of MCSN is, however, a testimony of the willingness and amenability of the Commission to hold high the interests and realities of right owners. It appears that it is this same right-owner reality that necessitated the nullification of the approval granted. At the end of the day copyright collective management is all about the people; the people who create content and those who exploit them.

It is apparent that some of the challenges a one time Director General of the Nigerian Copyright Commission referred to, after his recall from suspension for approving MCSN have been addressed by the courts. Other practical aspects still exist, however, which neither our learned counsels nor the collecting societies seem to have grasped. By this I mean the fact that the controversy about collecting societies has afforded the opportunity to unwilling users to refuse to pay for the use of content protected by copyright under the cloak of not knowing who to pay to (a situation brought about and sustained by reason of the controversies), resulting in creators not being compensated for usage of their works. On the other hand creativity is one way or the other stifled, and the revenue that could have accrued to the creators (nationally and internationally) which in turn would have significant impact on the nation's Gross Domestic Product (GDP)[147] is lost in the canal of the

---

[144] The lead judgment was delivered by Ibrahim Mohammed Musa Saulawa.

[145] CA/L/787/2008.

[146] Ibid.

[147] See generally, www.wipo.int/ipdevelopment/en/creative_industry/economic_contribution.html *Date of use*: 31 March 2012 where reference was made to a guideline used in measuring the economic contributions of the copyright and creative industries to the Gross Domestic Product of nations and their economy in general. It was noted that "Since its publication, a number of countries have successfully used the Guide and results demonstrate the substantive economic contribution of the creative industries in terms of their share in Gross Domestic Product (GDP), generation of employment and trade. The surveys show that the creative industries represent a dynamic sector which, on average, grows faster than the rest of the economy".

CMO crisis. The culture[148] of *pay for use,*[149] an intrinsic copyright culture[150] has become difficult and almost impossible to entrench in the minds of the public. This has thus brought about the enthronement of a free reign impression/mentality to the use of content in which copyright subsists. This no doubt is wrong but continues and will continue until the issues are addressed.

On the part of government, the continued crisis takes up unimaginable government time and resources. The several media smear campaigns against each other and against the Commission, to which the Commission must respond either to the supervising Minister or some other government official; and even more the distraction from other primary responsibilities are challenges the courts may not be in a position to capture. However, the voices of the crying authors continue to send out these vibes and it is clear that if these challenges are not addressed in a practical way, creativity in the music and entertainment industry may become a thing of the past.

The questions that therefore still linger before us are:

1. Would the collective administration system in Nigeria fare better without Sections 17 and 39 of the Nigerian Copyright Act?; and
2. Is the copyright industry in Nigeria actually benefiting from the heightened regulatory oversight of the Commission over collecting societies? If yes, the question has to be further asked as to why all the unending controversies. If no then we need to ask: Should Sections 17 and 39 be scrapped, reviewed or dealt with otherwise?

It is not my intention to answer these questions in this present work. I would however, like to end with two thoughts as captured in the words of William Patry in his book, Moral Panics *and the Copyright Wars*, and those of Frank Keating, in his foreword to the book *The Regulatory Craft* authored by Malcolm K Sparrow. Whatever one's view about the regulation of societies, I would suggest that these two thoughts present some useful food for thought.

> Copyright is suffering from an irrational exuberance that copyright owners will always act in their own best interests, and in acting in their own interests will automatically be acting in society's best interest too. But what is good for copyright owners is not always good for the country. As a monopoly, copyright vests copyright owners with an easy, government-created ability to act in anti-competitive and anti-innovative ways, ways that are harmful to the public interest...The copyright industries will act in the public interest only when

[148] See Lessig *Free Culture* xvi where he noted that a culture without property; or in which creators cannot get paid, is anarchy, not freedom.

[149] See Gustavo *Intellectual Property and Competition Law* 72 where he referred to the US Digital Millennium Copyright Act and the EU Information Society Directive and noted that the laws are aimed at 'codifying' in practice, a general principle of pay-per-use for all uses of all intellectual work distributed online.

[150] See the Preamble to the Statute of Anne (8 Anne. c. 19) where it was noted that the use without pay of the work of authors was "to their very great detriment, and too often to the ruin of them and their families", and based on the above and other reasoning, the Statute of Anne, the first Copyright Act was enacted on the 10th day of April 1710.

we insist that they do. Regulation is therefore a precondition to the copyright system functioning properly; regulation for the public interest should thus not be viewed as an exception, but as the norm.[151]

But although we need regulation, we do not need regulators who are", in Sparrow's words, "nitpicky, unreasonable, unnecessarily adversarial, rigidly bureaucratic, and incapable of applying discretion sensibly.[152]

---

[151] Patry *Moral Panics* 101.

[152] Sparrow *The Regulatory Craft* VIII.

Chapter 5
Conclusion: Nigerian Collective Management of Copyright: In the Right Direction or Going Amiss?

5.1 Introduction

In this work I set out to consider whether or not any merit exists in the continued existence of the current regulatory framework for collective management in Nigeria, and what the best operational framework for collective administration in Nigeria would be, taking into cognizance the legal battles that have ensued in the last 20 years and the many interventions by the government of Nigeria and other international organizations like the world intellectual property organization (WIPO) and the international confederation of societies of authors and composers (CISAC) to resolve the issues.[1]

In Chap. 1, I traced the evolvement of copyright, from its early recognition through the Statute of Anne and leading to the modern time. I did this within the context of showing how creativity in the very beginning displays similarities with the concept of copyright as we know it today, and the rationale for its recognition. In the same chapter, I traced the evolvement of the collective management organization structure and its use in the administration of copyright and related rights. In Chap. 2, I attempted to trace the evolution of the system of collective management in Nigeria, highlighting the influence of the British colonial rule in this regard. Chapter 3 explored the legal framework for collective management in Nigeria from 1911 to 1970 till the current legislation of 2004 as well as the regulations issued to give effect to the provisions of the Act. It also considered the nomenclature adopted by Nigeria for CMOs; the requirement for formation of a CMO; conditions for approval/granting of a licence; the core objectives and activities of CMOs; powers to make regulation to give effect to the provisions of the Act; issues relating to the single v multiple-rights society form; the issue concerning whether CMOs should be "for profit or not for profit" entities, and illegality/criminalization of carrying out the activities of a CMO without requisite approval. Chapter 4 highlighted the regulatory challenges of Collective Management in Nigeria, in this regard noting the lacuna of the 1988 Act, the challenges posed by the introduction of Sects. 17 and 39 to the Nigerian Copyright Act, as

[1] See Sect. 1.7.

O. Ola, *Copyright Collective Administration in Nigeria*, SpringerBriefs in Law,
DOI: 10.1007/978-3-642-35819-7_5, © The Author(s) 2013

well as the several legal contentions that have ensued as a result of the provisions of the above referred sections.

It is very obvious that the various issues emerging from the preceding chapters demand an answer to the question as to whether the present collective management regulatory environment in Nigeria is likely to lead to the desired haven. In this concluding chapter the intent is to attempt to answer this question and in this regard to make a comparative analysis of the Nigerian collective management regulatory environment and the nascent regulatory system of South Africa with a bid to determining whether the Nigerian CMO regulatory environment could borrow a leaf from the South African regime and conversely, to determine whether the South African regime could, itself be wanting and thus would borrow from the Nigerian position.

5.2 The Path to the New Regime

The reformation initiative for collective administration of copyright in Nigeria which commenced about the end of 2006 culminated in the issuance of a new regulation[2] for collective management organizations in Nigeria. The reform not only brought about the issuance of the regulation but by virtue of the regulation[3] and an application process that ensued, the copyright society of Nigeria (COSON) obtained approval from the Nigerian Copyright Commission and emerged as the sole collective management organization for musical works and sound recordings in Nigeria.[4] The approval granted COSON was heralded with jubilations in the Nigerian entertainment industry[5] and has been credited to team spirit, made possible by synergy built between different interest groups in the Nigerian entertainment industry to ensure that the approval was obtained.[6] By 20 May 2010

[2] On the 28th of September, 2007, the Copyright (Collective Management Organisation) Regulation 2007 was issued. It wasn't until the 3rd of October 2007 however that it was published in the official gazette as No.98 of Vol 94.

[3] Regulation 2 of the Copyright (Collective Management Organization Regulation) 2007.

[4] 2010-05-24 Monday The Guardian 3.

[5] See http://www.cosonng.com/stakeholders.html *Date of use*: 4 May 2012 where Tony Okoroji delivered a lecture at the Intellectual Property Law Association of Nigeria on Monday, 27 September 2010 at the Lagos Boat Club and said, "The COSON approval received wide jubilation from music industry stakeholders across the country. Quite a bit of champagne was popped to celebrate what many of us consider a historic event"; and the words of **Hon John Ewelukwa Udegbunam** who said, "The Nigerian Music Industry Coalition wishes to reaffirm its 100% support of the Federal Government approval of COSON, one of the most important developments in the Nigerian entertainment industry in the last 50 years".

[6] Ibid, where Okoroji noted that "for the first time in the history of the industry, nine key national associations, including Performing Musicians Association of Nigeria (PMAN), Nigerian Association of Recording Industries (NARI), Music Label Owners & Recording Industries Association of Nigeria (MORAN), Association of Music Business Professionals (AMB. PRO), Performing & Mechanical Rights Society (PMRS), etc., came together to request the approval of

when COSON was approved, the new collective management organization regulation had been publicly put to use and its regulatory powers over the collective administration sector in Nigeria had been asserted.

The application process was thrown open to the entire public by public notices calling for indications of interest,[7] an invitation to submit actual applications[8] and an extension of the deadline for submissions.[9] At the expiration of the extended deadline, three applications had been received from three interested organizations, namely; wireless application service providers Association of Nigeria LTD/GTE (WASP), musical copyright society Nigeria (LTD/GTE) (MCSN), and COSON (LTD/GTE). The Nigerian Copyright Commission in considering the application empanelled an in-house committee to assess the applications against the requirement of the Act, regulations, and the general public interest. The Committee met severally and made site visitations to the offices of the interested organizations. The Committee took cognizance of the need to set parameters for the consideration of the applications and was guided by the following:

1. "That applications would be considered for approval based on the statutory requirements for approval to function as a Collecting Society under the Copyright Act and the Regulations.
2. That beyond the statutory requirements, the Committee shall consider provisions in the internal rules of the applicants with a view to determining:
a. If such will promote transparent management of the Society;
b. If the Society guaranty participation of all categories of right owners in the music industry without discrimination; and
c. If the provisions are in any way contradictory or contrary to the provisions of the Copyright Act or the Regulations.
3. That the approval of the society would be in the overall national interest".[10]

Based on the above and after due consideration COSON emerged as the approved organization and consequently the sole collective management organization in

(Footnote 6 continued)
COSON. It gave the application a very big voice". See also Efe Omoregbe's comment when he said, "The coalition is a result of this conclusion that all of us—the "militant" stake-holders-have arrived at. COSON is a child of this coalition. COSON is the pathway to the resolution. Parochial interests within and without will try to subvert the process but they will fail because if there's one thing I am dead sure about, it's the fact that the people of the Nigerian music industry are TIRED of this RUBBISH—all the CMO, piracy rubbish MUST be cleared out. And the time is NOW".

[7] 2008-12-29 Monday, The Guardian.

[8] 2009-06-24 Wednesday, The Guardian.

[9] 2009-08-27 Thursday, The Guardian. See also the report of the CMO Assessment Committee where it was noted that "following a representation to the Commission by certain stakeholders in the music industry led by the Performing Musicians Association of Nigeria (PMAN) and other stakeholders, the Commission extended the deadline for submission of applications, from July 24th 2009, to December 31st 2009".

[10] Report of CMO Assessment Committee (Unpublished).

Nigeria for Musical works and Sound Recordings. It should be noted that COSON is not the sole collective management organization in Nigeria, as another collective management organization already existed in respect of *literary works.*[11] COSON's approval gives it sole authority to administer rights in Music Works and Sound Recordings.[12]

5.3 Regulatory Framework Bringing Hope

The amendments to the Copyright Act, first in 1992 and then in 1999 brought into Nigeria's collective administration regime, a regulatory dispensation[13] with criminal sanctions[14] on offenders and also limits the right to commence or maintain actions for infringement of copyright.[15] The amendments among other things set out conditions for establishing a collecting society,[16] the profit or nonprofit nature of a collecting society in Nigeria,[17] the issue of single or multiple societies,[18] and makes it mandatory for any organization which is to carry on the duties of negotiating and granting of licenses, collecting and distributing royalties to right owners, to first obtain approval from the Nigerian Copyright Commission as well as providing that failure to obtain such an approval by an organization carrying on the duties of a collecting society is an unlawful act.[19] It was further noted that to commence an action for infringement of copyright, any person carrying out the duties of a collecting society must represent more than 50 owners of copyright in any category of works protected by the Act.[20] The powers to make regulations to give effect to the purport of the enactment was also provided and

---

[11] Reproduction Rights Society of Nigeria (REPRONIG) is an approved collecting Society for Literary works.

[12] See http://www.cosonng.com/stakeholders.html where Okoroji noted that "By that announcement, COSON joined Reprographic Rights Organization of Nigeria (REPRONIG) which has been the sole copyright collective management organization for literary works in Nigeria".

[13] Introduced through Section. 39 Nigerian Copyright Act.

[14] Section 39(5) and (6) Nigerian Copyright Act.

[15] See Justice Obiageli's comments in *Compact Disc Technologies V MCSN* CA/L/787/2008 where she noted that "… compliance with this condition precedent to the institution of an action by any person carrying on business of negotiating and granting of license or persons collecting and distributing royalties in respect of copyright works is fundamental to the competency of the action and the court to proceed with the suit", and further noted that "s.17 of the Act does not, oust the subject matter jurisdiction of the court or derogation from the rights of the citizen, it only postpones the time for instituting a suit which means go and comply to the provision and get back to the court".

[16] Section 39(2) Nigerian Copyright Act.

[17] Section 39(2)b Nigerian Copyright Act.

[18] Section 39(3) Nigerian Copyright Act.

[19] Section 39(4) Nigerian Copyright Act.

[20] Section 17 Nigerian Copyright Act.

further to this provision, the Copyright (Collecting Societies Regulation) was issued in 1993 and repealed in 2007 when the Copyright (Collective Management Organizations) Regulation was issued and published in the official gazette of the Federal Republic of Nigeria. A detailed analysis on the provision of the Act and regulations has been given in Chap. 3.

The striking features of Nigeria's regulatory and operative structure for collective administration lies in its approval powers and the powers to limit actions for infringement of Copyright. The approval powers of the Commission is aptly captured in Section 39 (4) where it provides that "it shall be unlawful for any group of persons to purport to perform the duties of a society without the approval of the Commission as required under this section of this Act". The powers of limitation are provided in Section 17 of the Act, which provides that "no action for the infringement of copyright or any right under this Act shall be commenced or maintained by any person… unless it is approved under Section 39 of this act to operate as a collecting society or it is otherwise issued with a certificate of exemption by the Commission". As demonstrated earlier,[21] these two issues have thrown up several legal battles which have been resolved on the one hand in favor of the statutory provisions, thereby reaffirming that prior approval by the Nigerian Copyright Commission is required by any person or organization desirous of carrying on the duties of a collecting society[22] and that without such approval, no action may be commenced or maintained for Copyright infringement as the party doing so would lack the requisite locus standi.[23] On the other hand, it has also been held that the said approval is not required[24] and thus the right to commence and maintain actions against Copyright Infringement is unfettered since jurisdiction is not affected.[25] It has been observed that since the introduction and intervention by the Commission of its regulatory and oversight responsibilities over collective administration in Nigeria, there have been challenges particularly in the administration of rights in music works and sound recordings. The outcome of the problem has been the inability of right owners to be paid royalties for the exploitation of their works.[26] In contrast to the lingering problem, the newly approved collective management organization, COSON, in December 2011, was reported to have paid out royalties to the tune of N25.7 million to right owners.[27]

---

21 See Chap. 4 above.

22 MCSN V Adeokiin. Judgment given by Justice Ukeje.

23 *Compact Disc Technologies V MCSN,* supra.

24 MCSN V Adeokin supra On Appeal at the Court of Appeal.

25 See MCSN V Details Suit No. FHC/L/CS/934/95, MCSN v Guinness Suit No.FHC/L/CS/904/05, MCSN v Vee Networks FHC/L/CS/707/05.

26 See 2006-07-22 Saturday Punch A3.

27 See http://ynaija.com/2011/12/20/copyright-society-pays-nigerian-musicians-royalties-worth-millions/ where Chi Ibe noted that "The highlight of the meeting was the announcement that the sum of N25, 720, 588.20 was available for immediate distribution to all members of COSON whose names were on the society's register as at 19 May, 2011, if so approved by the AGM. The scheme was indeed approved by the members and the distribution started at the venue amidst

The Commission considers this as a sign of seriousness on the part of COSON and as such commended the organization for its proactive stance and its determination in ensuring that the core values of a collective management organization are maintained as well as pursuing the interest of right owners, as evidenced through the payment of royalties to right owners.[28]

5.4 Legal Framework for Collecting Societies in South Africa

5.4.1 Introduction

Having provided above a synopsis of the Nigerian position, it now becomes necessary to turn south and to consider the relevant position with regard to the collective management of rights in South Africa, with the aim of thereafter attempting a comparative analysis between the two systems.

The November 2009 High Court order for the liquidation of South Africa's third mechanical rights collecting society, South African Recording Association Limited (SARRAL)[29] has been reported as one of the reasons why the Department of Industry and Trade's decided to empanel a commission[30] to review the Copyright Laws of South Africa and particularly to assess the effectiveness of the structure of collecting societies in South Africa, including those that belong to

(Footnote 27 continued)
singing, dancing and jubilation as hundreds of musicians stood in line, collected their royalties peacefully and thanked the Almighty for witnessing the day when such could happen in Nigeria".

[28] See NCC Press release NCC/ADM.532/IPR23A 16-03-2012 where the Director General noted that "We are pleased to note that COSON, the organization representing right owners of music and sound recordings made its first royalty distribution to its members since its approval in 2010, in December 2011. We have monitored the performance of the organization and are satisfied with the present state of operations".

[29] The other two mechanical rights societies are the National Organization for Reproduction Rights in Music (NORM) and more recently, the Southern African Music Rights Organization (SAMRO) which is best known for its administration of performing rights, but ventured into the administration of mechanical rights in light of the difficulties faced by SARRAL.

[30] See http://www.billboard.biz/bbbiz/content_display/industry/news/3ic2e2b84001a6ce30186fc31ed5d54a5d *Date of use*: 16 April 2012 where Diane Coetzer reporting the South African probe on collecting societies reported that a retired Supreme Court judge, Judge Ian Farlam would chair the commission. It was also noted that "The retired judge will be assisted by five commissioners—ethnomusicologist and cultural researcher Professor Musa Xulu; former deputy minister of Social Development and policy analyst Jean Swanson-Jacobs; chartered accountant Nala Mhlongo; intellectual property lecturer Professor Tana Pistorius; and Oupa Leboga, secretary of the Creative Workers Union of South Africa. Public hearings, research and benchmark studies will be undertaken by Farlam and the five commissioners".

authors, composers, recording companies, musicians/artists and others.[31] The effectiveness of the structure of a collecting society is no doubt fundamental to the underlining aim for its existence as it holds in trust the rights of its members who earnestly await the harvest of their labor.[32]

South Africa like many other countries has in place structures for the collective management of copyright and related rights. Interestingly, the structure which has existed for over 50 years[33] was only recently subjected to regulation, which in itself is still largely restricted to public play rights.[34] This section of the work is intended to provide a brisk overview of the regulatory framework for collecting societies in South Africa and to attempt a comparison with the Nigerian regulatory framework for collecting societies.

5.4.2 Three Relevant Enactments to Collecting Societies in South Africa

A communal reading of the provisions of the Copyright Act 1978[35] at Sections 1(ix)[36] and (xxvii)[37]; 9A(1),[38] 39,[39] and Chap. 3[40]; as well as the Performers' Protection Act[41] at Sects. 1(1)[42] and 5(3)[43] and the Collecting Society Regulation[44] would constitute the legal framework for the establishment and operations of collecting societies in South Africa.[45]

---

[31] http://www.billboard.biz/bbbiz/industry/publishing/two-of-south-africa-s-largest-royalty-collection-1005161292.story *Date of Use: 16 April 2012.*

[32] See Reg 6(2) Collecting Society Regulation 2006, which provides for the aim of a collecting society and notes that the rights administered by a collecting society are rights entrusted to it by the right holders.

[33] Southern African Music Rights Organization (SAMRO) is a collecting society in South Africa established in 1961 and is still in operation till date.

[34] See Section 1(iii) Collecting Society Regulations 2006 where at the interpretation section of the regulation it was noted that "*public playing right* means the right of a right holder to receive a royalty in terms of Section 9A of the Copyright Act, 1978, and/or the right to receive a royalty in terms of Section 5(l)(b) of the Performers' Protection Act, 1967, as the context dictates".

[35] Copyright Amendment Act, No. 9 of 2002.

[36] Meaning of collecting society.

[37] Defining a licensing scheme.

[38] Royalties.

[39] Powers of the Minister to make regulations.

[40] Copyright Tribunals.

[41] The 2002 Act was an amendment to the Performers' protection Act 11 of 1967.

[42] Meaning of collecting society.

[43] Restriction on the use of Performances.

[44] Collecting Society Regulations GN 517.

[45] Regulation 2 Collecting Society Regulations 2006.

A collecting society under South African Law has been defined as a collecting society established under the Act.[46] The Act gives no further definition of the term but it can be inferred from the functions of licensing bodies as stipulated in the Act, that collecting societies are involved in granting licences against agreed terms and conditions as to charges and tariffs.[47]

The aim of a collecting society is to administer[48] public playing rights[49] efficiently and effectively and to maximally exploit the rights entrusted to it by right holders.[50] These rights as they relate to royalties[51] are focused on the broadcast of a sound recording, causing the transmission of the sound recording in a diffusion service, and communicating the sound recording to the public.[52] The Copyright Act 1978 contemplates that a royalty has to be paid in respect of the exploitation of sound recordings, public play rights, unless the parties agree otherwise.[53] This royalty payment should be determined by agreement between the user of the sound recording, the performer and owner of the copyright, or between their collecting societies.[54] Where however, the said agreement cannot be reached the matter may be referred to the Copyright Tribunal[55] by the user, performer, or copyright owner.[56] Where the rights are administered by a collecting society, at least 80 % of the royalties collected are to be distributed to right holders, and not more than 20 % is to be used for the cost of administering the rights by the collecting society.[57]

Persons or licensing bodies desirous of acting as representative collecting societies and representing 50 or more copyright owners,[58] performers[59] or both[60];

---

46 See S.1 (ix) Copyright Act 1978 which defines collecting society. This section was inserted by S.1 (a) of Act 9/2002. This definition is also contained in the Performers' Protection Act 11 of 1967 and the Collecting Society Regulations 2006.

47 S.1 (xxvii) Copyright Act 1978. Reference to licensing bodies is in respect of Chap. 3, which provides for a Copyright Tribunal.

48 Regulation 6(2) Collecting Society Regulations.

49 Regulation 1 Collecting Society Regulations 2006 defines a public playing right as "the right of a rightholder to receive a royalty in terms of Section 9A of the Copyright Act, 1978, and/or the right to receive a royalty in terms of Section 5(1) (b) of the Performers Protection Act 1967, as the context dictates".

50 Regulation 6(2) Collecting Society Regulations 2006.

51 Section 9A(1)b &(2)b Copyright Act 1978; S.5(3)a&(4)a of the Performers Protection Act, No. 11 of 1967 as amended in 2002 and Regulation 3 of the Collecting Society Regulations 2006.

52 This is also referred to as needle time or public play rights.

53 S.9A(1)a Copyright Act 1978.

54 S.9A (1)b Copyright Act 1978.

55 See S.29(1) Copyright Act 1978 and as stipulated by the Arbitration Act, 1965.

56 S.9A(1)c Copyright Act 1978.

57 Regulation 6(2).

58 Regulation 3(1)a Collecting Society Regulations 2006.

59 Regulation 3(1)b Collecting Society Regulations 2006.

60 Regulation 3(1)c Collecting Society Regulations 2006.

or organization(s) representing 50 or more copyright owners, performers, or both, in respect of the right to receive payment of royalties for public playing rights as contemplated in Section 9A of the Copyright Act 1978 and Section 5 of the Performers' Protection Act are required to obtain accreditation from the Registrar[61] in order to be authorized to function as a collecting society.[62] The process for accreditation is by means of a written application lodged with the Registrar who has the discretion to grant or deny the application.[63] The registrar in considering the application is expected to satisfy himself/herself that

a. it appears from the particulars supporting the application and the information considered that the applicant is able to ensure adequate, efficient and effective administration throughout the Republic of the rights to be entrusted to the collecting society for administration;
b. membership is open to copyright owners or their licensees and/or to performers whose rights the applicant seeks to administer and/or to organizations representing such copyright owners or licensees and/or performers;
c. the applicant affords to copyright owners or their licensees and/or to performers, or to organizations representing copyright owners or licensees and/or performers an appropriate right and opportunity to take part in decision making concerning the affairs of the applicant and the administration of the rights in question, as well as the distribution of royalties to be received;
d. the applicant is able to comply with the obligations set out in these Regulations (Chap. 2);
e. the person or persons appointed as representatives, managers, and members of the governing body of the applicant are fit or proper persons to act as such and are in their majority South African citizens or permanent residents;
f. the principal place of business in respect of rights administered in the Republic is situated in the Republic;
g. the accreditation of the applicant does not conflict with, undermine or diminish the adequate, efficient, and effective administration of the right to receive payment of a royalty in terms of Section 9A of the Copyright Act, 9978, or Section 5(l) (b) of the Performers' Protection Act, 1967, as undertaken by a collecting society already accredited and established under the Copyright Act, 1978.[64]

An accreditation is granted for a term of 5 years and is renewable for further periods of 5 years.[65] The collecting societies are expected to invite the registrar to annual or special general meetings of the members and are to provide annual

[61] Registrar means the Registrar of Copyright at the Companies and Intellectual Property Registration Office (CIPRO). See Regulation 1(iv) Collecting Society Regulations 2006.

[62] Regulation 3(1) Collecting Society Regulations 2006.

[63] See Regulations 3(2), (3), and (4).

[64] Regulation 3(3)a–g Regulation 5 Collecting Society Regulations 2006.

[65] Regulation 5 Collecting Society Regulations 2006.

activity reports containing information about its activities, financial records, and such other records as may be necessary to assess the degree of compliance of the collecting society against the provisions of the relevant enactments.[66] They are expected to furnish specific information to the registrar including the following:

a. "copies of the memorandum and articles of association, trust deed, founding documents, articles of incorporation, reciprocal agreements with foreign collecting societies, or any similar document setting out the basic organizational structure of the collecting society, including the name and address of its auditors;
b. notice of any amendments or changes to the documents referred to in paragraph 4(3)(a), together with a report setting out succinctly the reasons for the amendment or change;
c. tariffs set by the collecting society for potential users or user groups, and any amendments thereto;
d. annually, an up-to-date list of members;
e. annually, an up-to-date list of agreements with foreign collecting societies;
f. annual audited financial statements; and
g. any documentation or report that the Registrar may reasonably require".[67]

Licensing arrangements are provided for between collecting societies and users. In the event of an agreement being reached between a collecting society and users, the agreed tariff may be jointly submitted to the Registrar for publication in the gazette. Where however, an agreement is not reached, users are free to apply the provisions of Chap. 3 of the Copyright Act 1978 by approaching the Copyright Tribunal or through referral to arbitration.[68] In the circumstance that users are dissatisfied with the tariff set by collecting societies but wish to use works administered by the collecting societies, such users may pay the amount set by the collecting society into an escrow account pending the determination by the copyright tribunal or arbitration.[69]

5.4.3 Comparing South Africa and Nigeria

The introduction in 2002 of the amendments to both the Copyright Act of 1978 and the Performers' Protection Act together with that of the Collecting Societies Regulation—a regulation made pursuant to the powers vested in the Minister of Trade and Industry in consultation with the Minister of Finance—for the estab-

[66] Regulation 4(2) Collecting Society Regulations 2006.

[67] Reg 4(3) a–g.

[68] Reg 7(4) Collecting Societies Regulations 2006.

[69] Reg 7(5) Collecting Societies Regulations 2006.

lishment, composition, funding, and functions of collecting societies contemplated in Section 9A[70] ushered in, for the first time, a regulatory dispensation for collecting societies in South Africa. This dispensation is, however, only applicable to public play rights leaving the more popular rights—performing and mechanical rights—outside the purview of the current regulatory regime.

As indicated above, the regulatory framework for collecting societies in South Africa is fairly new. The framework enables the supervision of collecting societies and the protection of the interests of right owners, users, as well as collecting societies. It has a number of similarities with the framework that exists in Nigeria. Its oversight responsibility for accreditation[71] of collecting societies is similar to Nigeria's approval oversight functions on collecting societies.[72] Both regulations provide for application,[73] revocation,[74] tenure and renewal,[75] membership structure,[76] licensing,[77] distribution,[78] settlement of disputes,[79] escrow/holding accounts,[80] limitation on administrative cost,[81] and obligation to furnish information[82] among several other possible similarities. On the other hand, the major differences between both frameworks lie in the coverage of rights administered and in the nature and consequences of the authorization granted to applicants to operate (**accreditation** for South Africa and **approval** as applied by Nigeria).

---

[70] See Section 39 (cA) Copyright Act 1978 [Check this reference. It is not correct]. I just did and it appears to be the right one. The only thing was that I did not include the brackets initially. You are right. It is the one in which you placed the footnote that confused me. I have added 'See' to clarify.

[71] Reg 3 Collecting Society Regulations 2006.

[72] Section 39 of the Nigerian Copyright Act.

[73] See Reg 3(1) of the Collecting Society Regulations 2006 for South Africa and S.39 (1) Nigerian Copyright Act and Reg 1 of the CMO Regulation 2007.

[74] See Reg 3(6) of the Collecting Society Regulations 2006 for South Africa and Reg 2 of the CMO Regulation 2007 for Nigeria.

[75] See Reg 3(5) of the Collecting Society Regulations 2006 for South Africa and Reg 1(9) and Reg 3 of the CMO Regulation 2007 for Nigeria.

[76] See Reg 5 of the Collecting Society Regulations 2006 for South Africa and Part II of the CMO Regulation 2007 for Nigeria.

[77] See Reg 7 of the Collecting Society Regulations 2006 for South Africa and Reg 13 of the CMO Regulation 2007 for Nigeria.

[78] See Reg 8 of the Collecting Society Regulations 2006 for South Africa and Reg 15 of the CMO Regulation 2007 for Nigeria.

[79] See Reg 7(4) & (5) of the Collecting Society Regulations 2006 for South Africa and Reg 14 of the CMO Regulation 2007 for Nigeria.

[80] See Reg 7(5) & (6) of the Collecting Society Regulations 2006 for South Africa and Reg 11&12 of the CMO Regulation 2007 for Nigeria.

[81] See Reg 6 of the Collecting Society Regulations 2006 for South Africa and Reg 10 of the CMO Regulation 2007 for Nigeria.

[82] See Reg 6 of the Collecting Society Regulations 2006 for South Africa and Reg 4 of the CMO Regulation 2007 for Nigeria.

5.4.4 Coverage of Rights Administered

While the regulatory framework in South Africa narrows down to regulating the administration of needle time or public playing rights,[83] that is, the right of public performance of a musical work as well as a sound recording the Nigerian regulatory framework for copyright and related rights covers all works and rights without any exclusions. The reasoning for South Africa's exclusion from regulatory supervision of the more traditional rights such as rights of reproduction (mechanical) and performing of *musical works* in public ("performing rights", which include the right to broadcast the musical works and to transmit them in a diffusion service) could be imagined and linked to several reasons: political and economic and probably, logical.

On the political and economic end, subtle pressure is often mounted by interest groups, in this instance, groups such as performing rights organizations (PRO's) and possibly the International Confederation of Societies of Authors and Composers (CISAC) to take steps to dialogue either formally or informally with agencies, departments, ministries, and in fact individuals in government to ensure that the policy thrusts of such governments conform with certain specific economic interests and agendas to the end that no interruption is brought to the status quo.[84] The resultant effect of these pressures and interests are the introduction or further developments or policies either in favor of or against such interests. But as was noted by Dr Williams in his goodwill message at the CISAC African Committee meeting held in Madagascar, "the primary consideration for the approval of a collecting society should be the interest of the members that the society is intended to serve."[85] Dr Williams' opinion was that the policy thrust of a government with regard to collective administration of copyright and related rights should always place the national interest at the fore and ensure that whatever pressures and interests are expressed are balanced against this national interest.

On the logical end, one could reason that the prior established and smooth existence of such organizations may have conveyed a salient message, *that the sector has established an efficient and effective mode of operation; that it is thus now on "auto cruise" and would not need the intervention, or better still the disruption of government in that area.*[86]

---

[83] See Reg 6(2) Collecting Society Regulations 2006 which provides that the aim of a collecting society shall be to administer public playing rights.

[84] See Dr. Williams, Goodwill Message, Meeting of African Committee on CISAC, Madagascar, Nov 21-24 2000 where he noted that "Understandably, the PRS in its own response had shown concern about the status of MCSN and in fact requested that consideration be given to ensuring that MCSN is registered with the [Commission] as soon as the rules and regulations come into force. But as I had hinted above, the primary consideration for the approval of a collecting society should be the interest of the members that the society is intended to serve".

[85] Ibid.

[86] SARRAL's liquidation is however a disincentive to that reasoning.

Whatever the perspective, be it the political/economic or logical one, the underlining interest ought to be the national interest. I would therefore submit that if the restricted coverage of rights administration to public playing rights alone actually serves the national interest of South Africans, then the current framework is in the right direction and must be applauded and emulated. If, however, the national interest of South African right holders are not adequately, effectively and efficiently captured, protected and guaranteed, it then becomes apparent that the current regulatory framework is inadequate in that regard. Similarly, if the all inclusive nature of rights administration of copyright and related rights, serve the national interest of Nigerians it can be assumed that the current regulatory framework is in the right direction but if otherwise, not so.

Notwithstanding the above, it is my view that Nigeria's legal provisions for the regulation and administration of CMO's appear stringent but nonetheless suitable for Nigeria and Nigerians considering the level of development of most Nigerians.[87] The challenge I see is not altogether with the law (I say altogether because although I believe the legal provision is a rich one, it is nonetheless stringent as it purports to limit the right of action of an organization carrying out the activities of a collecting society without the approval or exemption of the Commission), but with those saddled with the responsibility of implementing and exercising the powers conferred by the law. The exercise of discretion in favor of a single society model for CMOs in Nigeria may have contributed to the prolonged crises that have ensued in the collective administration sector of Nigeria. The national interest for Nigeria in my view would be the enthronement of an enabling environment for a thriving creative industry which would allow for proper remuneration in the most effective and efficient way for creators while at the same time providing adequate balance in the interest of the public. Although a single model structure had been advocated by the WIPO consultant as noted in Chap. 4, it is my view that considering the Nigerian circumstances the exercise of discretion in favor of multiple societies for the same work or rights would have brought a viable solution to the Nigerian crisis and would thus have enabled a platform for rewarding right owners for creativity.

---

[87] See the *Human Development Report* pages 1–2, available at http://hdrstats.undp.org/images/explanations/NGA.pdf Date of Use: 9th May 2012 where it was noted that Nigeria's Human Development Index value and rank for 2011 was 156 out of 189 countries and territories whilst in 2010 it was 146 out of 169 countries. It was further noted that "The HDI is a summary measure for assessing long-term progress in three basic dimensions of human development: a long and healthy life, access to knowledge and a decent standard of living. …a long and healthy life is measured by life expectancy, access to knowledge is measured by: i) mean years of adult education, which is the average number of years of education received in a life-time by people aged 25 years and older; and ii) expected years of schooling for children of school-entrance age, which is the total number of years of schooling a child of school-entrance age can expect to receive if prevailing patterns of age-specific enrolment rates stay the same throughout the child's life. Standard of living is measured by Gross National Income (GNI) per capita … To ensure as much cross-country comparability as possible, the HDI is based primarily on international data from the UN Population Division, the UNESCO Institute for Statistics (UIS) and the World Bank".

On the part of South Africa, the liquidation of SARRAL prompts me to hold the view that the non inclusion of other copyright and related rights outside the needle time right leaves right owners at risk. I am therefore of the view that a restricted regulatory regime as that of South Africa has the potential of leaving the right owners at the mercy of the administrators of copyright and related rights, and woe betides the right owners if the administrators are of the caliber that led SARRAL.

5.4.5 Authorization to Operate

The other issue borders on the nature and implication of the authorization granted to applicants desirous of performing the functions of a collecting society. Applicants who are so desirous in South Africa and satisfy the Registrar are granted accreditation.[88] In Nigeria, however, applicants who satisfy the conditions of the Commission are granted an approval.[89]

An accreditation (South Africa) provides the legal platform on which an interested organization can act as a collecting society for needle time or public play rights. Regulation 3(1) makes it unlawful for a collecting society representing 50 or more right owners and/or performers to do so without accreditation. It has however been observed that no sanctions are provided by the regulation against an organization acting as a collecting society without accreditation.[90] It may be a mirage to obtain optimal efficiency in any system unless effective control mechanisms are put in place to support the regulatory framework.[91] This is so because the natural inclination of man is to be free and possibly do whatever he wishes. This was noted by Thomas Hobbes[92] in his popular work *Leviathan*, when he opined that human beings are naturally selfish and wicked and that government was created to protect people from their selfishness and wickedness. In his popular quote he noted that "giving power to the individual would create a dangerous situation that would start a *war of every man against every man* and make life *solitary, poor, nasty, brutish, and short*."[93] Thomas Hobbes' opinion highlights the possibilities that an unchecked system can create. He was of the view that clear control was necessary to keep humans in check. Dean however argues that the Registrar who is charged with ensuring the proper functioning of this genre of collecting societies is entitled to seek an interdict[94] from the court against an errant

---

[88] Reg 3 Collecting Society Regulations 2006.

[89] Section 39 Nigerian Copyright Act.

[90] Dean *Handbook of Copyright* 7.5.15.

[91] Adewopo *Nigerian Copyright System: Principle and Perspectives* 128.

[92] He was born in 1588 and in 1651 he wrote his most influential and popular work, "Leviathan".

[93] http://www.rjgeib.com/thoughts/nature/hobbes-bio.html: *Date of Use: 18 April 2012.*

[94] Reg 4(4) b Collecting Society Regulations 2006.

collecting society.[95] However, a careful reading of the entire provision of Reg 4 and particularly Reg 4(4) (a) and (b) in my opinion is directed at collecting societies that have already been accredited and not to organizations' operating as collecting societies without accreditation. The option to withdraw the collecting society's accreditation as contemplated at Reg 4(4) (a) signifies that the collecting societies in question are those already within the regulatory purview of the enabling enactment.

In Nigeria, the grant of an approval to an applicant desirous of carrying on the duties of a collecting society provides the needed legality for such applicants.[96] Any person or organization purporting to carry on the duties of a collecting society without the prior approval of the Commission is in contravention of the law and such acts have been clearly labeled unlawful[97] and attract a fine of N1,000 on the first conviction and for any other subsequent conviction, a fine of N2,000 or to imprisonment for a term not exceeding 6 months or to both such fine and imprisonment.[98] In the case of a corporate body the fine is N10,000 on the first conviction and N2,000 for each day on which the offence continues.[99]

This supervisory and regulatory role of the Nigerian Copyright Commission **to approve** has been the subject of many a litigation.[100] In *Musical Copyright Society of Nigeria (Ltd/Gte) (Plaintiff) V Guinness Nigeria Plc (Defendant/Applicant),*[101] the defendants contended that the plaintiff lacked the prerequisite *locus standi* to demand royalties from them because it had not been approved as a collecting society by the Nigerian Copyright Commission. It noted further that the Commission which is responsible for granting approvals had not approved the plaintiff and thus the demand from the defendant was illegal and a violation of the copyright Act. The plaintiff relied on the Nigerian Copyright Act which permits the owner, assignee, or an exclusive licensee of the copyright to commence or institute an action for infringement of copyright. The plaintiff therefore contended that it was not a collecting society but an owner, assignee, and exclusive licensee in which capacity it had commenced the suit. The court holding in favor of the plaintiff noted that the defendants contested the authorization of the Commission as against the rights specifically conferred by the Nigerian Copyright Act and that the defendants were not actually challenging the Plaintiff's right as owners, assignee, and exclusive licensee, neither were they complaining that the breach was not actionable. The court therefore held that in-so-far as the Plaintiff was the

---

95 Dean, Op Cit at footnote 90.

96 Section 39 Nigerian Copyright Act.

97 Section 39(4) Nigerian Copyright Act.

98 Section 39(5) Nigerian Copyright Act.

99 Section 39(6) Nigerian Copyright Act.

100 See *Musical Copyright Society of Nigeria (Ltd/Gte)* (Plaintiff) V Guinness Nigeria Plc (Defendant/Applicant) Suit No.FHC/L/CS/904/2005 at page 2 paragraph 4(f) where the defendant noted "That the NCC had prior to now institute[sic] many criminal actions against the Plaintiff for acting illegally and most of the actions are still pending in courts".

101 Suit No.FHC/L/CS/904/2005.

owner/assignee and exclusive licensee, the plaintiff had the requisite *locus standi*. The defendant's objections were therefore accordingly dismissed. The reasoning of the judge was not unique as it was predicated on an earlier court of appeal case, *MCSN Ltd/Gte V Adeokin*[102] where the judge gave a similar judgment, which has also been reaffirmed in a very recent case between *MCSN V Nigerian Copyright Commission*[103] and in a ruling delivered in 2007 by Justice I.N Auta.[104]

On the flip side, the courts[105] have also affirmed the approval powers of the Nigerian Copyright Commission over organizations carrying out the duties of negotiating and granting of licenses as well as collection and distribution of royalties. In the *Adeokin Case* referred to above, at the Federal High Court level prior to its going on appeal, Justice Ukeje held that "looking at the totality of the evidence presented by the plaintiff it is no doubt a collecting society within the meaning of Section 32B of the Copyright Act"[106] and therefore required the approval of the Nigerian Copyright Commission to operate, and having not obtained the said approval, lacked the *locus standi* to institute the suit. A similar ruling was given in the same court by Justice I.M Sani in *Musical Copyright Society of Nigeria Ltd/Gte V. Nigerian Copyright Commission.*[107] At the court of appeal level, a similar judgment was also given in *Compact Disc Technologies Ltd V Musical Copyright Society of Nigeria Ltd/Gte*[108] where Regina Obiageli Nwodo (J.C.A) gave a consenting judgment and noted that the right to institute proceedings in a court of law for redress or assertion of a right enforceable at law is not unlimited; and that S.17 of the Nigerian Copyright Act has stipulated a condition precedent, that is, any person carrying on the business of negotiating and granting of licenses, collecting and distributing royalties is required to obtain approval from the Commission. In this regard she noted, "S.17 does not oust the subject matter jurisdiction of the court or derogate from the rights of the citizen, it only postpones the time for instituting a suit which means go and comply to [sic] the provisions and get back to the court."[109]

As can be clearly seen from the cases above, the issue of the Commission's approval powers has been highly debated in the court and there appears to be no consensus by the courts on this issue. The legal provision of the law as to approval is conspicuously spelt out in the Nigerian Copyright Act. The interpretation of the law by the judiciary has, however, thrown up challenges to the Commission's regulatory and supervisory role to collecting societies in Nigeria.

---

[102] CA/L/498/97.

[103] Suit No: FHC/L/CS/35/2008.

[104] *Musical Copyright Society Nigeria Limited v Vee Network Limited* (Trading under the name and style "V Mobile Nigeria") Suit No: FHC/L/CS/707/05.

[105] At both Federal High Court and Court of Appeal.

[106] Suit No: FHC/L/CS/216/96.

[107] Suit No: FHC/L/CS/478/2008.

[108] Appeal No: CA/L/787/2008.

[109] Ibid.

It appears to me that the legal framework as provided by Nigeria encapsulates that of South Africa and goes further to cover all rights of right holders and furthermore, provides clear sanctions to infractions of the provisions contained in the legal framework. In this regard, the Nigerian legal framework for collective administration of copyright and related rights may be preferred to that of South Africa.

5.5 Lessons for Africa

On the whole, it is clear that regulations are essential for public peace and order and for our mutual convenience. It is therefore wise to prohibit human behavior that threatens our collective existence and benefits. Society has a right and an obligation to act collectively through government to prevent others from engaging in fraudulent business practices, and in doing so the regulator should be motivated by the pursuit of the national interest. We must however guard against regulators who are "nitpicky, unreasonable, unnecessarily adversarial, rigidly bureaucratic, [and] incapable of applying discretion sensibly"[110] because they frustrate the intent of the framework, and eventually destroy what they are meant to build. Justice Archibong in *Musical Copyright Society of Nigeria and 4 others v Nigerian Copyright Commission and 4 others* captured the essence of the above statement when he noted that

> the Copyright Commission was established to reinforce the rights of copyright owners, assignees and licensees; not to be an institutional hurdle with arbitrary powers to restrict the private enjoyment and enforcement of such rights. Copyright owners do not exist at the pleasure of the Copyright Commission; or merely to validate its establishment. And most definitely the Copyright Commission was not established to undermine, denigrate or exact obeisance from copyright owners… The Copyright Commission and its principal officers should not be in the business of subverting the property rights of copyright owners[111]

The lessons to be drawn from Nigeria's regulatory and operational mechanisms for collective administration of copyright and related rights can be culled from its comprehensive legal framework—a framework which has led to the several legal battles referred to above and to which divergent decisions have been reached. The following will be important to note for the future of collective administration in Nigeria and indeed Africa.

1. The need for supervisory and regulatory agencies of government to seek the national interest above all others in taking and making decisions is to be upheld;
2. The role of the Judiciary in establishing a balanced supervisory and regulatory framework should not be underestimated; neither can it be over emphasized, taking cognizance of the esoteric nature of Copyright and other Intellectual

110 Sparrow *The Regulatory Craft* VIII.

111 Suit No: FHC/L/CS/35/2008 at pages 18 & 19.

Property fields. To this end there is the need for training and continuous learning for judges as well as to ensure that judges with cognate experience and knowledge are placed to adjudicate over copyright issues.

3. The need to take caution in the adoption of Western models and to reassess our current regulatory strategies against our socioeconomic and cultural ideals with a mind to adopting strategies that can interface with the Western culture and are yet representative of our intrinsic nature and values, is to be particularly noted.
4. For Nigeria specifically, the country may need to look inward and ask why collective administration for musical works and sound recording has been entangled in this battle for over 20 years. A careful analysis of the battle will show that virtually all the court cases have something to do with the Musical Copyright Society of Nigeria Ltd/Gte. Regulators may therefore wish to exercise their discretion in the interpretation and use of Section 39(3) of the Nigerian Copyright Act and consider the possible advantages of multiple collecting societies for one class of copyright owners. With time, market forces will determine what is in the right owners' best interest. What should not be allowed to continue is a situation where regulators continue to hold tenaciously to a supposed ideal situation whereas right owners are living in abject poverty, not being able to receive remuneration for their creativity due to an avoidable collapse in the collective administration of their copyright and related rights.

Table of Cases

1. *Musical Copyright Society Nigeria Ltd/Gte v Adeokin Records* Suit No: FHC/L/CS/216/96; also reported as (2007) 13 NWLR Part 1952, 615
2. *Musical Copyright Society Nigeria Ltd/Gte V Adeokin* CA/L/498/97 (Court of Appeal)
3. *Compact Disc Technologies V Musical Copyright Society Nigeria Ltd/Gte* CA/L/787/2008
4. *Musical Copyright Society Nigeria Ltd/Gte V Details* FHC/L/CS/934/95
5. *Musical Copyright Society Nigeria Ltd/Gte V Nigerian Copyright Commission*:- FHC/L/CS/35/2008
6. *Musical Copyright Society Nigeria Ltd/Gte V Nigerian Copyright Commission*:- Suit No: FHC/L/CS/683/94
7. *Nigerian Copyright Commission V Musical Copyright Society Nigeria Ltd/Gte* CA/L/925/2011
8. *Musical Copyright Society Nigeria Ltd/Gte v Nigerian Copyright Commission*:- Suit No: FHC/L/CS/478/2008
9. *Performing Mechanical Rights Society Ltd/Gte V Nigerian Copyright Commission*:- Suit No: FHC/L/CS/61/2007
10. *Prof Nwaoboshi & 4 ors V The Military Governor of Delta State & 2 0rs* (2003) 11 NWLR (Part 831) 305 at 310
11. *Layanju V Araoye* (1959) SC NLR 416.
12. *Nafiu Rabiu Vs. The State* (1981) 2 NCLR P. 293 at 362
13. *Agbakoba Vs. Director SSS* (1984)6 NWLR PT.351 P.475 at 499–500
14. *Medical and Health Workers Union of Nig V Honorable Minister of Labour and Productivity*:- (2005) 17 NWLR PT.953 P.120 at 155.
15. *Musical Copyright Society of Nigeria (Ltd/Gte) V Guinness Nigeria Plc* Suit No.FHC/L/CS/904/2005
16. *Musical Copyright Society Nigeria Limited v Vee Network Limited* (Trading under the name and style "V Mobile Nigeria") Suit No: FHC/L/CS/707/05
17. *MCSN v Nigeria Hotels* Suit No FHC/L/43/89

O. Ola, *Copyright Collective Administration in Nigeria*, SpringerBriefs in Law,
DOI: 10.1007/978-3-642-35819-7,

Newspaper

Kolapo and Oduntan 2006-07-22 Saturday Punch A3
Kolapo Y and Oduntan O "Steps you must take to avoid your work being pirated-DG, NCC" 2006-07-22 Saturday Punch A3

NCC 2008-12-29 Monday, The Guardian
Nigerian Copyright Commission "Call for indication of interest from interested organizations" 2008-12-29 Monday, Guardian

NCC 2009-06-24 Wednesday, The Guardian
Nigerian Copyright Commission "Invitation for application for approval to operate a CMO" 2009-06-24 Wednesday, Guardian

NCC 2009-08-27 Thursday, The Guardian
Nigerian Copyright Commission "Extension of deadline for submission of application to operate a CMO" 2009-08-27 Thursday, Guardian

NCC 2010-05-24 Monday, The Guardian
Nigerian Copyright Commission "Approval of Collecting Society of Nigeria" 2010-05-24 Monday The Guardian 36

NCC Press Release 2012-03-16
Nigerian Copyright Commission Press Release; Ref: NCC/ADM.532/I/PR23A "Commission commends COSON for the payment of royalties"

O. Ola, *Copyright Collective Administration in Nigeria*, SpringerBriefs in Law,
DOI: 10.1007/978-3-642-35819-7,

Unpublished Papers

Adewopo "Collective Administration"
Adewopo A "Collective Administration in the Music Industry" (Unpublished position paper prepared to provide rationale for the approval of a second collecting society for Music in Nigeria 6th May 2005 Abuja) 1–4

Kendrick "Grand Performing Rights"
Kendrick J "Grand Performing Right Licensing in the United States" (Unpublished paper delivered at the 42nd Edition of the International Television Festival Golden Prague 7–11 May 2005 Prague) 1–61

Nigerian Copyright Commission "Collective Administration"
Nigerian Copyright Commission "Collective Administration in the Music Industry" (Unpublished position paper presented to the Honorable Attorney General of the Federation and Minister of Justice Abuja August 16, 2010) 1–49

Williams S.O "Goodwill Message"
Williams S.O "Goodwill Message" (Unpublished paper delivered at the Meeting of African Committee of CISAC, Nov 21–24 2000, Madagascar) 1–5

O. Ola, *Copyright Collective Administration in Nigeria*, SpringerBriefs in Law,
DOI: 10.1007/978-3-642-35819-7, © The Author(s) 2013

Unpublished Report

CMO Assessment REPORT: Report of Collective Management Organisation Assessment Committee (unpublished).

O. Ola, *Copyright Collective Administration in Nigeria*, SpringerBriefs in Law, DOI: 10.1007/978-3-642-35819-7, © The Author(s) 2013

Bibliography

Books

Adewopo *Nigerian Copyright System*

Adewopo A *Nigerian Copyright Systems Principles and Perspectives* (Odade Lagos 2012)

Adewopo *Proposals for Liberalisation of Collecting Societies in Nigeria*

Adewopo A "Proposals for Liberalisation of Collecting Societies in Nigeria" in Asein J.O and Nwauche E.S (eds) *Decade of Copyright in Nigeria* (Nigerian Copyright Commission Abuja 2002)

Boldrin and Levine *Against Intellectual Monopoly*

Boldrin M and Levine DK *Against Intellectual Property* (Cambridge University Press New York 2008)

Carrol *Intellectual property rights*

Carrol MC "A Framework for Tailoring Intellectual Property Rights" Kur A and Vytautas M (eds) in *The structure of Intellectual Property Law* (Edward Elgar Cheltenham 2011)

Dean *Handbook of Copyright*

Dean OH *Handbook of South African Copyright Law* (Juta & Co Cape Town 2006)

Dinwoodie *One size fits all*

Dinwoodie GB "Remarks: "One size fits all" consolidation and difference in intellectual property law" Kur A and Vytautas M (eds) in *The structure of Intellectual Property Law* (Edward Elgar Cheltenham 2011)

Ferguson Empire

Ferguson N *Empire The Rise and Demise of the British World Order and the Lessons for Global Power* (Basic Books, New York 2004)

Fitzgerald et al *OAK Law Project*

Fitzgerald B et al *Open Access to Knowledge Law Project Report No.1* (Department of Education Science and Training Brisbane 2006)

DOI: 10.1007/978-3-642-35819-7, © The Author(s) 2013

Fiscor *Collective Management*

Fiscor M *Collective Management of Copyright and Related Rights* (WIPO Publication No.855 (E) Geneva 2002)
Ficsor M *Collective Administration of Copyright and Neighboring Rights* (WIPO publication No. 588 (E) Geneva 1990)

Garnett, Davies and Harbottle *Copyright*

Garnett K, Davies G and Harbottle G (eds) *Copinger and Skone James on Copyright* 15th ed (Thomson Sweet & Maxwell London 2005)

Gervais *Collective Management*

Gervais DJ *Collective Management of Copyright and Neighbouring Rights in Canada: An International Perspective* (Department of Canadian Heritage Canada 2001)

Gustavo *Intellectual Property and Competition Law*

Gustavo G *Intellectual Property and Competition Law: The Innovation Nexus* (Edward Elgar Publishing Limited Cheltenham 2007)

Hugenholtz and Okediji *Limitation and Exceptions*

Hugenholtz PB and Okediji RL *Conceiving an International Instrument on Limitations and Exceptions To Copyright* (Open society Institute New York 2008)

Holy Bible

The Holy Bible, King James Version (Zondervan Publishers New York 1985)

Lessig *Free Culture*

Lessig L *Free Culture: The Nature and Future of Creativity* (Penguin Books New York 2004)

Litman *Copyright Non-Compliance*

Litman J "Copyright Non-Compliance (Or Why We Cant "Just Say Yes" to Licensing" Merges RP and Ginsburg JC (eds) in *Foundations of Intellectual Property* (Foundation Press New York 2004)

Ndongko Africa Spectrum

Ndongko *WA Indigenisation Policy and the Development of Private Enterprise in Nigeria.* (Africa Spectrum Hamburg 1980)

Okoroji *Copyright*

Okoroji T *Copyright Neighbouring Rights & The New Millionaires* (Tops Lagos 2008)

Park *The Sources of Nigerian Law*

Park AEW *The Sources of Nigerian Law* (Sweet & Maxwell Sydney 1963)

Patry *Moral Panics*

Patry W *Moral panics and the Copyright Wars* (Oxford University Press, New York 2009)

Shyllon *Intellectual Property Law in Nigeria*

Shyllon F *Intellectual Property Law in Nigeria* (Max Planck Institute for Intellectual Property, Competition and Tax law, Munich 2003) Vol. 21

Sparrow *The Regulatory Craft*
Sparrow MK *The Regulatory Craft Controlling Risks, Solving Problems and Managing Compliance* (The Brooking Institution, Washington D.C 2000)

Uchtenhagen *The Setting-up of New Copyright Societies*
Uchtenhagen U *The Setting-up of New Copyright Societies Some Experiences and Reflexions* (WIPO Publication No. 926(E) Geneva 2005)

Journal/Articles

Engle 2008 35 N.Ky.L.Rev 1
Engle E, "Aristotle law and justice: The tragic hero" 2008 (35) *N.Ky.L.Rev* 1–17

Gervais 2008 5:1&2 UOLTJ 1
Gervais DJ "Making copyright whole: A principled approach to copyright exceptions and limitations" 2008 (5:1&2) UOLTJ 1–41

Gervais 2011 COLUM-VLA J.L & ARTS 427
Gervais DJ "The landscape of collective management schemes" 2011 (34.4) COLUM-VLA J.L & ARTS 423–449

Mihaly 1997 NAMTA (22) 60
Mihaly C "Flow and Creativity", 1997 (22) NAMTA Journal 60–97

Veljko 1980 University of Ljubljana, Yugoslavia Sage Journal 1
Veljko R "Positive and Negative Power: Thoughts on the Dialectics of Power" 1980 (1) Institute of Sociology, University of Ljubljana, Yugoslavia Sage Journal 3–19

Internet

Anon www.wipo.int/ipdevelopment/en/creative_industry/economic_contribution.html Date of use: 31 March 2012

Anon "Publishing industry responses to Hargreaves explain why copyright remains at the base of our creative industries" http://copyright-debate.co.uk/?p=667 (Date of Use: 14 March 2012)

Anon http://www.wipo.int/about-ip/en/about_collective_mngt.html (Date of use: 6 March 2012)

"**Anon Thomas Hobbes**" http://www.rjgeib.com/thoughts/nature/hobbes-bio.html: (Date of Use: 16 April 2012)

Anon "Wright Brothers" http://www.notablebiographies.com/We-Z/Wright-Brothers.html#b (Date of use 23 April 2012)

Anon "Wright Brothers: Biography Life, story, death, school, young, information, born, contract, house, time" http://www.notablebiographies.com/We-Z/Wright-Brothers.html#b#ixzz1tOF89iMB (Date of use: 23 April 2012)

Anon "Introduction To Collective Management Of Copyright And Related Rights" http://uatm.com.ua/laws/int/Introduction%20to%20Collective%20Management%20of%20Copyright%20and%20Related%20Rights.pdf Date of use: 14 March 2012)

Anon "Comparison of Rights in the Copyright Bundle" http://faculty.ist.psu.edu/bagby/Comparison%20of%20Rights%20in%20the%20Copyright%20Bundle.pdf: (Date of use 12 April 2012)

Asif T "Judicial Precedent" http://www.lawteacher.net/PDF/Judicial%20Precedent.pdf (Date of use: 5 May 2012)

Coetzer D "South African Probe Into Collecting Societies" http://www.billboard.biz/bbbiz/content_display/industry/news/e3ic2e2b84001a6ce30186fc31ed5d54a5d (Date of use: 16 April 2012)

Coetzer D "Two of South Africa's Royalty Collection Agencies Join Forces" http://www.billboard.biz/bbbiz/industry/publishing/two-of-south-africa-s-largest-royalty-collection-1005161292.story (Date of Use: 16 April 2012)

David du Pless "Compliance Copyright Act and Performers' Protection Act Part 1" http://www.sampra.org.za/downloads/asa_sep_08.pdf: (Date of use: 23 March 2012)

Drexl J "Collecting Societies and Competition" http://193.174.132.100/shared/data/pdf/drexl_-crmos_and_competition.pdf (Date of use: 31 March 2012)

Gervais DJ "ELECTRONIC RIGHTS MANAGEMENT AND DIGITAL IDENTIFIER SYSTEMS" http://www.wipo.int/edocs/mdocs/enforcement/en/acmc_1/acmc_1_1 main1.pdf (Date of use: March 6 2012)

Gervais DJ "The Landscape of Collective Management Schemes" http://works.bepress.com/daniel_gervais/35/ (Date of use: 6 March 2012)

Gervais DJ http://www.wipo.int/edocs/mdocs/enforcement/en/acmc_1/acmc_1_1main1.pdf. (Date of use: 13th March 2012)

Hargreaves report "Independent Review of IP and Growth" available online at http://www.ipo.gov.uk/ipreview.html (Date of use 24 March 2012)

HM Government "Government's response to the Hargreaves review" available online at http://www.bis.gov.uk/assets/biscore/innovation/docs/g/11-1199-government-response-to-hargreaves-review (Date of use: 24 March 2012)

Hugenholtz PB and Okediji RL "Conceiving An International instrument On Limitations And Exceptions To Copyright" (P. Bernt Hugenholtz and Ruth L. Okediji) Available online at http://www.ivir.nl/publicaties/hugenholtz/finalreport2008.pdf (Date of use 4 April 2012)

Iain S "Why Copyright is still important after 300 years" http://copyright-debate.co.uk/?p=424: (Date of use: 14 March 2012)

Ibe C "Send Down the Naira Rain! Fashek, Onyeka Onwenu and Others get Royalties Worth Millions" http://ynaija.com/2011/12/20/copyright-society-pays-nigerian-musicians-royalties-worth-millions/ (Date of use: 10 March 2012)

IFFRO http://www.ifrro.org/members/reproduction-rights-society-nigeria (Date of use: 21 March 2012)

King James Bible*available* online at http://www.kingjamesbibleonline.org (Date of use: 16 May 2012)

Lamont A "Great Creation Scientists: The Wright Brothers Pioneers of the Skies" http://www.answersingenesis.org/articles/cm/v13/n4/wright (Date of use: 12 May 2012)

Levesque LC "Breakthrough Creativity" http://www.leadershipnow.com/creativityquotes.html Date of use 23 April 2012)

LongfellowWH "A psalm of Life" http://www.potw.org/archive/potw232.html (Date of use: 7 February 2012)

Newton I "Standing on the shoulders of Giants" http://en.wikiquote.org/wiki/Isaac_Newton (Date of use: 26 January 2012)

NORCODE http://www.norcode.no/en/links/(Date of use: 21 March 2012)

Okoroji T and Omoregbe E "Stakeholders Parliament" http://www.cosonng.com/stakeholders.html (Date of Use: 16 April 2012)

Parry R "The Changing Role of Copyright" http://copyright-debate.co.uk/?p=159 (Date of Use: 14 March 2012)

PwC report "An economic analysis of copyright, secondary copyright and collective licensing. Available online at http://www.ipo.gov.uk/ipreview-c4e-sub-plsreport.pdf (Date of use: 24 March 2012)

UNDP "Human Development Report" available at http://hdrstats.undp.org/images/explanations/NGA.pdf

University of Melbourne Copyright Office "The Music Licence" http://www.unimelb.edu.au/copyright/information/musiclicence.html (Date of use: 10 March 2012)

WIPO "Collective Management of Copyright and Related Rights" http://www.wipo.int/about-ip/en/about_collective_mngt.html (Date of use: 6 March 2012)

Legislation

African Charter

African Charter on Human and Peoples Rights (OAU Doc. CAB/LEG/67/3 rev.5; 1982 (21) ILM 58)

Berne Convention

Berne Convention for the Protection of Literary and Artistic Works (Paris Act of July 24, 1971) as amended on (September 28, 1979)

CMO Regulation

Copyright (Collective Management Organization) Regulation 2007 issued in the Official Gazette on the (3rd of October, 2007) as No.98 of Volume 94.

Copyright (Dispute Resolution Panel) Rules

Copyright (Dispute Resolution Panel) Rules, 2007 Issued on the 2nd October 2007, Government Notice No.66 Volume 94

CAMA

Companies and Allied Matters Act 1990

Collecting Societies Regulation

Copyright (Collecting Societies) Regulation 1993
Collecting Society Regulations (GN 517) 2006,

Nigerian Copyright Act

Nigerian Copyright Act Cap C28 Laws of the Federation of Nigeria **2004**.
Nigerian Copyright Act Cap 68, Laws of the Federation of Nigeria **1990**. Copyright Decree No. 61 of **1970**. Copyright Act, **1911**. Nigerian Copyright (Amendment) Decree No 98 of **1992**. Nigerian Copyright (Amendment) Decree No 42 **1999**

Performers' Protection Amendment Act

Performers' Protection Amendment Act Government Gazette No. 8 of 2002 at Vol. 444 No. 23555 Cape Town 25 June 2002. Performers' Protection Act 11 of 1967

Rome Convention

Rome convention, 1961 International Convention for the Protection of Performers, Producers of Phonograms and Broadcasting Organisations done at Rome on October 26, 1961

MIX
Papier aus verantwortungsvollen Quellen
Paper from responsible sources
FSC® C105338

If you have any concerns about our products,
you can contact us on
ProductSafety@springernature.com

In case Publisher is established outside the EU,
the EU authorized representative is:
Springer Nature Customer Service Center GmbH
Europaplatz 3, 69115 Heidelberg, Germany

Printed by Libri Plureos GmbH
in Hamburg, Germany